外国人に日本を説明するための

たった**3語**の
マジカルフレーズ

300

アンドリュー・ロビンス[著]

岡本茂紀[編・訳]

300 Magical
Three-Word
English Phrases

IBCパブリッシング

カバーデザイン ＝ 菊池　祐

著者イラスト ＝ 長崎祐子

はじめに

　初めて本書の構想を出版社と話し合ったとき、私の頭の中には1つの明確なフレーズがありました。undercover sex lodge です。私の中では抱腹絶倒ものの楽しいフレーズで、「ラブホテル」という言葉の意味を凝縮した究極の3語フレーズでした。とはいえ、皮肉にも私は、17年も日本に暮らしたというのに、いまだに一度もラブホテルに足を踏み入れたことがないのですが。考えてみれば、日本人ではない私は、本書で取り扱っている多くの言葉について、しばしば「のれん」に視界を遮られながら、よそ者の立場で記述したような気がします。「義理と人情」のように、日本文化を深く理解していないとなかなかピンとこないようなコンセプトもあり、多くの場合、自分の知識や経験に頼るのではなく、独自に調べたり、辛抱強い編集者と相談したりしなければなりませんでした。そうは言っても、もちろん、「親父ギャグ」のように事実上、世界共通の言葉もあります。ところで、今夜は豚肉のしょうが焼きの材料を買いに走らなくてはいけないのです。面倒だけど「しょうがない」（すみません）。

　本書を読むに当たって、1つ念頭に置いておくべきことがあります。それは、ほとんどの場合、あるコンセプトを完璧に伝えるには3語では足りないということです。これは外国語の語句を説明する場合に限ったことではありません。ときには、同じ母語の話者同士でもコンセプトを伝えられないことがあります。単に、それが言語というものの性質なのです。コミュニケーションを取るということは、信号を出力するということで、あとはその信号がこちらの期待どおりに受け取られるよう願うしかありません。そして多くの場合、そううまくはいかないのです。私たちが意図したとおりに気持ちを通わせることができないというのは、人間が経験する中で最大の悲劇の一つです。いや、申し訳ありません！　少々深刻になりすぎましたね。私がここで言い

たいのは、本書で取り上げている3語フレーズは、会話を進めるためには非常に優れているということです。これらのフレーズを口に出せば、相手の好奇心や質問を誘うことにつながり、やり取りがとても面白いものになる上、お互いに新たな発見があるでしょう。それこそが、本書の「マジカル」な部分なのです。

　いつものように、この出版プロジェクトを実現させてくれた人たちに感謝の意を表したいと思います。辛抱強く見守ってくれた上に貴重な意見を述べてくれた、編集者兼翻訳者の岡本さんとディレクターの京子。紆余曲折の中、私がキャリアの道筋を開く手助けをしてくれたメンターの洋とニャンゴタニ。そしてもちろん、揺るぎないサポートをしてくれた家族の皆──アミ、ノア、カイル、サラ、パパ、ママ、アレックス、ミッシー、デイブ、ジョナス、ライアン、マイキー、ニコ、アニー。愛しています。そして、心の底から感謝しています。

アンドリュー・ロビンス

アメリカ人の視点で日本を再発見する
本書の構成と活用法

　「英語で日本を説明する」ことは、昔から日本の英語学習者にとってなじみ深い課題の一つです。身近な事柄についてなら知識があるし勘も働くから、肩肘張らずに英語で話せるはずだ、というわけです。ところが、実際にやってみると、これがそう簡単ではないことに気づかされます。最初に突き付けられるのが、私たちは実は自分の国やその文化について大して知らず、理解もしていないという現実です。そしてもう一つ、例えよく分かっていることでも、それを異文化の人々に伝わりやすいシンプルで的を射た英語に置き換えて説明するのは思いのほか難しい、という問題も立ちはだかっています。特に後者は、個々の日本の事象についての知識を深めたり、英語の語彙力を拡充したりすれば済むような、単純な話ではありません。こうした問題を解決するには、何らかの発想の転換が必要です。

　相手にとって未知の、あるいはなじみの薄い文化について効果的に説明するには、実は、逆にこちらが相手の文化についての知識や理解を深めることも重要になってきます。どんな説明なら相手が受け入れやすいのかを考える上で、相手の文化的視点に立つことには意味があるのです。異文化間には、違いばかりではなく、似た点や共通項もあります。それに気づけば発想が転換され、相違点を説明するために類似点や共通点を利用する、という方策が現実味を帯びてきます。

　著者のアンドリュー・ロビンス氏は、生粋のアメリカ人でありながら、17年に及ぶ日本在住経験を持ち、日本人顔負けの流暢な日本語を操ります。本書では、そんな「日本人よりも日本をよく知るアメリカ人」アンドリューが、アメリカ人としての文化的フィルターを通して日本文化の森羅万象を眺め、そこから300の事象を選び、それぞれのエッセンスをコンパクトな3語フレーズで表現しています。アメリカ人の

視点で日本の事象を分析した結果、同胞のアメリカ人たちの腑に落ちる300のマジカルフレーズが生まれたのです。

　以下に、本書の基本構成と、各構成要素の効果的な活用方法を紹介します。

●日本文化を10のカテゴリーに分類

　本書は、Chapter 1「Food / Cooking　食事・料理」からChapter 10「Expressions　表現・言い回し」まで、10のカテゴリーに分けて章立てされています。Chapter 10では例外的に「いただきます」や「お疲れさまでした」など日本語特有の慣用的な言い回しを取り上げていますが、それ以外の章では、日本の文化・社会に見られる事物やコンセプトを表す日本語を分野別に整理し、英語の3語フレーズや説明文・例文などとともに掲載しています。Chapter 1から順番に読み進めるのもいいですし、興味のある分野から優先的にページをめくるのもいいでしょう。

●マジカルフレーズとその使い方をチェック

　各見出しの日本語の直下に、3語から成るマジカルフレーズと、それをあえて日本語に再翻訳したものを掲載してあります。再和訳文を見て、なぜこの日本語がこの3語フレーズになるのかを確認・実感してみてください。

　「文で説明してみよう！」には、当該の日本語を辞書的・事典的に説明する、短い英文を掲載しています。実際の会話場面では、例えばまず3語フレーズを披露し、その補足説明としてここにある英文を添える、といった使い方を想定することも可能です。

　「3語フレーズを会話で使おう！」には、当該のフレーズを用いた例文が掲載されています。もちろん、実際の会話の中で使うための練習素材として活用できます。しかし、著者のアメリカ人としての視座が

投影された文も数多く含まれているので、異文化的視点を学ぶための材料としても役立つはずです。

●各章の前半は背景説明付き

　各章前半の5または10項目（Chapter 10では全項目）には、著者によるエッセー風の背景説明文、Andrew's Pointが付してあります。ここには、各見出しの3語フレーズを考案するに至った背景説明や、それらの言葉・事象・コンセプトに関する著者の個人的な体験談などがつづられています。各章前半部には、著者の思い入れの強い項目が集められているとも言えます。分からないところは対訳で意味を確認しながら、著者のアメリカ人としての視点を共有するつもりで読んでみてください。

　なお、巻末の索引は、本書を辞書的に使いたいときに便利です。本文中では各項目をランダムに並べてあるので、特定の言葉が頭に浮かび、それの3語フレーズを調べたいと思ったときには、索引を当たるのが早道です。

　本書には、英語を異文化間コミュニケーションのツールとして捉えたとき、何に注意し、どんな点に目を向ければいいかのヒントが詰まっています。加えて本書は、アメリカ人の視点を通して日本文化を再発見する機会を提供するものでもあります。本書を、ぜひ語学力プラスαの向上に役立ててください。

編者・訳者　岡本 茂紀

目次

●音声一括ダウンロード●

本書の朗読音声（MP3形式）を下記URLとQRコードから無料でPCなどに一括ダウンロードすることができます。

https://ibcpub.co.jp/audio_dl/0795/

※ダウンロードしたファイルはZIP形式で圧縮されていますので、解凍ソフトが必要です。

※MP3ファイルを再生するには、iTunes（Apple Music）やWindows Media Playerなどのアプリケーションが必要です。

※PCや端末、ソフトウェアの操作・再生方法については、編集部ではお答えできません。付属のマニュアルやインターネットの検索を利用するか、開発元にお問い合わせください。

Chapter

1

Food/Cooking
食事・料理

お通し

compulsory restaurant appetizer
強制的な飲食店の前菜

文で説明してみよう！

An *otōshi* is a small, compulsory appetizer that acts in lieu of a cover charge.

お通しとは、サービス料の代わりの少量な強制的な前菜のこと。

３語フレーズを会話で使おう！

Some travelers resent having to pay for a **compulsory restaurant appetizer**, but I welcome the opportunity to eat something new that I might not have otherwise ordered.

旅行者の中には、お通しにお金を払わなければならないことに憤慨する人もいますが、私はふだん注文しないような新しいものを食べる機会を歓迎しています。

Andrew's Point

The first time I had *otōshi* at a restaurant in Japan, I was confused. When I went to pay, I saw the price and said, "What? Why do I have to pay for this? Sure it was delicious, but I didn't order it!" Obviously, I was unfamiliar with the custom. That's why "compulsory" is an essential part of the explanation. As for "restaurant," I wanted to make it clear that this wasn't something you might be required to eat when, say, dining at a friend's or relative's house. I cannot imagine the situation where a friend or relative would say to me, "You must eat this or I will not serve you the next dish!"

初めて日本のレストランでお通しを食べたとき、私は戸惑いました。お金を払おうとして、値段を見て「え？　なんでこれにお金を払わなきゃいけないの？　確かにおいしかったけど、注文してないのに！」。むろん、私はその習慣を知りませんでした。だから **compulsory** は説明の必須項目です。**restaurant** については、例えば、友人や親戚の家で食事をするときに食べなければならないものではない、ということをはっきりさせたかったのです。友人や親戚から、「これを食べないと次の料理を出さないよ！」と言われる状況は想像できませんから。

かき氷

delicately shaved ices

繊細に削られた氷

 文で説明してみよう！

Kakigōri is ultra-thin shaved ices flavored with syrup, often topped with condensed milk, and paired with red bean paste, ice cream, or a variety of other ingredients.

かき氷とは、シロップで味付けした極薄のかき氷のことで、練乳をかけたり、あんこやアイスクリーム、その他のさまざまな食材と組み合わせたりする。

 ３語フレーズを会話で使おう！

Regular old snow cones don't hold a candle to the rich flavors and fine textures of **delicately shaved ices**.

普通の昔ながらのスノーコーンは、かき氷の豊かな風味ときめ細かい食感にふさわしくありません。

Andrew's Point

Actually, there is a food similar to *kakigōri* in the U.S. It is called shaved ice, and it comes in a cone-shaped paper cup. It is not the same as in Japan, where you go into a restaurant, order it, and it comes out in a glass bowl. The flavors are also markedly different from those in Japan. There is no *matcha* green tea or *azuki* beans, of course. However, I think the biggest difference between Japanese shaved ice and American shaved ice is the fineness of the ice. American shaved ice is much more coarse-grained. In contrast, Japanese shaved ice is extremely thin and very fine. I used the word "delicately" to describe this difference.

実は、かき氷によく似た食べ物はアメリカにもあるのです。shaved ice と言って、円錐状の紙コップのようなものに入って出てきます。日本のように、店に入って注文し、きちんとガラスのボウルに盛られて出てくるようなものではありません。フレーバーも日本のものはずいぶん違いますね。抹茶とかアズキなんて、もちろんありません。とはいえ、日本のかき氷とアメリカの shaved ice の一番の違いは、氷の細やかさにあると思います。アメリカの shaved ice は、もっとジャリジャリして、氷の粒が粗い感じです。それに比べて日本のかき氷の氷は、極薄でとてもきめ細やかです。この違いを delicately という単語で表現しました。

たい焼き

fish-shaped pastry waffle
魚形ペーストリーワッフル

 文で説明してみよう！

Taiyaki, literally translated as "baked sea bream," is a baked sea-bream-shaped cake with a filling such as red bean paste.

たい焼きは、直訳すると「焼いたタイ」だが、タイの形をした焼き菓子で、あんが詰めてある。

 ３語フレーズを会話で使おう！

Convenience store premade **fish-shaped pastry waffle** is nothing compared to a freshly baked one, with its steaming hot filling combined with a slight crunch to the cake.

コンビニの出来合いのたい焼きは、焼きたてのたい焼きとは比べものになりません。本来、蒸し焼きにされた熱々のあんと、少し歯ごたえのある皮が組み合わさっているのです。

Andrew's Point

My first thought for *taiyaki* was "fish-shaped waffle cake," but that doesn't convey the idea that there's something else on the inside, not to mention that "waffle" renders "cake" slightly redundant. I then thought the idea of a "fish-shaped waffle pocket" sounded fun but was perhaps too ambiguous. Does the fish have a pocket? Do you put the fish in your pocket? Adding "pastry" made it clear that there was another element on or in the cake. I wasn't such a fan of *taiyaki* until a Swedish friend convinced me to try the *taiyaki* at Yamato Saidaiji station in Nara. The texture of those *taiyaki* can't be beat: they've found the perfect balance of crispiness and softness, almost like a French canelé. If I had room for a fourth word, I might try to get away with "soft-and-crispy."

たい焼きで最初に思いついたのはfish-shaped waffle cake でしたが、これでは中に何か入っているというイメージが伝わりません。言うまでもなく、waffle と cake では少々冗長ですし。次に、fish-shaped waffle pocket というアイデアも面白そうだと思ったのですが、曖昧すぎるかもしれません。魚にポケットがあるのか？ 魚をポケットに入れるのか？ pastry を加えることで、ケーキの上か中に別の要素があることを明確にできました。スウェーデン人の友人に奈良の大和西大寺駅のたい焼きを食べるように説得されるまで、私はたい焼きがそれほど好きではありませんでした。あのたい焼きの食感はたまりません。サクサク感と柔らかさのバランスが絶妙で、まるでフランスのカヌレのようです。もし4つ目の単語を入れる余地があるなら、soft-and-crispy を使えば何とか通じるかもしれません。

だし

god of stock

煮出し汁の神

文で説明してみよう！

Dashi is a family of broths made from steeping a variety of ingredients such as *konbu*, *shiitake* mushrooms, and bonito flakes in water.

だしは、昆布、シイタケ、かつお節など、さまざまな食材を水に浸して作る煮出し汁の一種。

３語フレーズを会話で使おう！

Strict vegetarians have a hard time traveling through Japan, given the ubiquitousness of **god of stock** in Japanese cuisine.

厳格なベジタリアンは日本を旅行するのが大変です。日本料理にはだしが付き物だからです。

Andrew's Point

In my house, I use *dashi* every day, whether it's just part of the *miso* soup or if it's been included it in *soborodon* or *gyūdon* or some other *don*—I make a lot of ●●*don*. If I wanted to aim for accuracy, I might've chosen something a little more tame like "fish kelp stock." But my motivation here was to convey how extraordinary *dashi* is and how essential it is to Japanese cuisine. I was also partly influenced by a fun 1996 Hong Kong comedy film called *God of Cookery*, wherein a know-nothing celebrity chef learns the true meaning of what it means to cook.

わが家では、毎日だしを使います。みそ汁はもちろんのこと、そぼろ丼や牛丼などの丼物にもです。正確さを優先するなら、**fish kelp stock**など、もう少し無難な表現にする手もあったかもしれません。でも、だしがいかに素晴らしいもので、日本料理に欠かせないものであるかを伝えたかったのです。また、1996年の香港の『食神』という楽しいコメディー映画の影響もあります。

ちらしずし

005

vinegared rice medley

酢飯メドレー

文で説明してみよう！

Chirashizushi is a bowl of *sushi* rice topped—or mixed in some regions—with ingredients such as raw fish, egg, and seaweed.

ちらしずしとは、酢飯の上に生魚や卵、のりなどの具材を乗せた——地方によっては混ぜた——丼のこと。

3語フレーズを会話で使おう！

Ryōko looked at the dish suspiciously—unlike the **vinegared rice medley** back home in Tokyo, the one she got in Osaka had all of the ingredients mixed together.

リョウコはけげんそうに、その食べ物を見つめました——東京のちらしずしと違って、大阪のちらしずしは具が全部混ざっていたからです。

Andrew's Point

I had two issues coming up with the three-word phrase for *chirashizushi*. The first issue has to do with regional differences. In Kanto, the seafood is prepared on top of the rice, while in Kansai, the seafood is mixed in with the rice. The second issue I had was how to differentiate *chirashizushi* from *kaisendon*. In the end, I decided that that particular distinguishing characteristic—vinegared rice—was important enough to encompass two-thirds of the phrase. I finished the phrase off with "medley" to avoid having to make the distinction between seafood on or in the rice. I could have used "assortment," but "medley" makes the dish sound more fun and enticing like a musical ensemble.

ちらしずしの3語フレーズを考えるにあたり、2つ問題がありました。1つ目は地域性の違い。関東では魚介類がご飯の上に乗っているのに対して、関西では魚介類はご飯に混ぜ込んであります。2つ目の問題は、ちらしずしと海鮮丼をどう区別するかということです。結局、酢飯という特徴が、フレーズの3分の2を占めるほど重要だと考えるに至りました。ご飯の上に魚介類が乗っているのか中に混ぜ込まれているのかを区別せずにすむように、medley でこのフレーズを締めくくりました。assortment でもよかったのですが、medley のほうが音楽アンサンブルのように楽しく魅力的な響きをこの食べ物に与えてくれます。

デパ地下

basement foodie paradise
地下の食べ物天国

文で説明してみよう！

Depachika, a portmanteau of "depāto" (department store) and "chika" (basement), is a department store basement upscale foodstuff market full of everything from confections and baked goods to obscenely priced fresh fruit and alcohol.

デパ地下とは、「デパート」と「地下」の合成語で、デパートの地下にある高級食材市場を指し、お菓子や焼いた食品から、とんでもない値段の新鮮な果物やお酒まで、何でもそろっている。

3語フレーズを会話で使おう！

I could spend a month in the **basement foodie paradise** and never run out of new foods to try.

デパチカで1カ月過ごしても、試すべき新しい食べ物が尽きることはありません。

Andrew's Point

I didn't want to leave "department store" out of the three-word phrase, but I found the other elements made for a more intriguing set. A "foodie paradise" brings to mind delicacies as far as the eye can see, while "basement" adds a certain shadowy allure. Of course, you know *depachika* in Japan are not shadowy in the slightest—they're generally clean, welcoming, and, most of all, delicious. I always recommend that visitors to Japan visit a *depachika* or two. You can eat 100 different things on 100 different days, and there will still be more things waiting for you to try. It is, without a doubt, a foodie paradise.

department store を3つの単語から外したくはなかったのですが、他の語を使ったほうがより興味深いフレーズになることに気づきました。foodie paradise は、見わたす限り多種多様なごちそうを思い起こさせ、basement は、ある種の謎めいた魅力を加えます。もちろん、日本のデパ地下は少しも謎めいてなどおらず、概して清潔かつ快適で、何よりもおいしさにあふれているわけですが。私はいつも、日本を訪れる人にデパ地下を1、2カ所訪れることを勧めています。100日あれば100通りのものを食べられるし、それでもなお食べてみるべきものが待ち受けているでしょう。間違いなく、食の天国です。

懐石料理

multi-course haute odyssey

多重コース料理の高級長旅

文で説明してみよう！

Kaisekiryōri is traditional full-course haute cuisine often served at Japanese inns and upscale restaurants.

懐石料理は、旅館や高級料亭でよく出される伝統的なフルコースの高級料理のこと。

3語フレーズを会話で使おう！

With two toddlers and a baby in the house, the prospect of getting away for a luxuriant dining experience with **multi-course haute odyssey** is little more than a dream.

2人の幼児と1人の赤ん坊がいる家庭では、高級懐石料理を楽しむために遠出するなんてほとんど夢物語です。

Andrew's Point

Up until just before we published, this item was "multi-course haute cuisine." The "multi-course" is obvious. The "haute" gives it a sense of refinement. And the "cuisine" makes it clear that it is a style of cooking. But I decided that "multi-course" was indication enough that we were dealing with food, and I wanted to squeeze in a little "spice," so to speak. I felt "odyssey" conveyed the idea of a romantic journey for your palate, which is how I feel about *kaisekiryōri*. I remember the first time I was treated to a fairly upscale *kaisekiryōri* experience. The food, the ambiance, the service—together, they made it one of those milestone moments that elevated my understanding of both Japanese cuisine and the potential of food in general.

掲載直前まで、この項目は **multi-course haute cuisine** でした。**multi-course** は当然として、**haute** は洗練された感じを与えます。そして **cuisine** で料理のスタイルを指すことが明確になります。でも、**multi-course** でこれが料理であることが十分に分かるので、いわばちょっとした「趣」を加えたいと思いました。**odyssey** を使えば、味を求めるロマンチックな旅といった意味が伝わると感じました。初めて高級な懐石料理を食べたときのことを覚えています。料理、雰囲気、サービス——それらが一体となって、日本料理と食全般の可能性に対する私の理解を深めてくれた、重要な瞬間の一つでした。

居酒屋

008

Japanese tapas bar

和風タパスバー

 文で説明してみよう！

An *izakaya* is a type of casual bar-restaurant that serves both alcoholic beverages and a variety of small dishes à la a tapas bar.

居酒屋は、アルコール飲料とタパスバー風の小皿料理の両方を提供するカジュアルなバーレストランの一種。

 ３語フレーズを会話で使おう！

The first thing I tend to order at a **Japanese tapas bar**—after beer, of course—is a serving of pork and kimchi.

居酒屋で私がよく最初に注文するもの ── もちろんビールの後での話ですが ── は、豚肉とキムチの盛り合わせです。

Andrew's Point

The first time I went to a tapas bar was in the early 2000s in Bethesda, Maryland—my hometown. I remember eating small dish after dish after dish. There was such a variety that I have no recollection of what I ate. I only remember the gluttony. Of course, the atmosphere of a tapas bar is different from your typical *izakaya*, which is why I added "Japanese." I was conflicted about that, however. In this book, I tried avoiding using "Japanese" in the three-word phrases as much as possible because "Japanese" applies to everything. After all, this is a book steeped in Japanese culture! But in this case, I found it important to make the distinction that this was not a Spanish tapas bar but was instead uniquely Japanese.

初めてタパスバーに行ったのは、2000年代の初め、私の故郷であるメリーランド州ベセスダでのことでした。次から次へと小皿料理を食べたのを覚えています。種類が豊富すぎて、何を食べたかまったく覚えていません。覚えているのは大食いしたことだけ。もちろん、タパスバーは日本の典型的な居酒屋とは雰囲気が違うので、ここでは Japanese を加えたのです。ただ、それにあたっては迷いがありました。というのも、この本では3語の中に Japanese という語を極力使わないようにしているからです。何しろ日本文化にどっぷり浸かった本ですから！　でもこの場合は、スペイン風のタパスバーではなく、日本独自のものであることを区別することが重要だと思いました。

立ち食いそば屋

stand-and-go soba stall

立ったまま食べ、すぐに出ていくそば屋台

文で説明してみよう！

Tachiguisobaya, literally translated as "stand and eat *soba*," are standing-only dining establishments that serve *soba*—and often *udon* as well—found in a variety of places, including train stations, commercial districts, and sports stadiums.

立ち食いそば屋は、直訳すると「立って食べるそば屋」で、駅や商業施設、競技場などさまざまな場所でそばを――たいていはうどんも――振る舞う、立ち食いのみの飲食店こと。

3語フレーズを会話で使おう！

Some may pine for Michelin-starred haute cuisine, but I'm happier filling my belly surrounded by urban bustle at a train station **stand-and-go soba stall**.

ミシュランの星を獲得した高級料理に憧れる人もいるかもしれませんが、私は都会の喧騒に包まれた駅の立ち食いそば屋で腹を満たすほうが幸せです。

Andrew's Point

I wanted to capture the four S's of *tachiguisobaya*: the *soba*, the standing, the speed, and the space (I decided to leave out the noisy fifth s: the slurping). "Soba," of course, stays as is. "Stand-and-go" makes it clear that no one is simply idling around, having a long chat with a neighbor—people are hustling and bustling. The space was a tough one. I almost went with "compartment" to convey that people are often squeezed tightly together, but I ultimately decided that "compartment" makes *tachiguisobaya* seem like a closed space, which doesn't feel right, even when there's a *noren*. Stall brings to mind a more open establishment.

立ち食いそばの4つのS、つまりsoba、standing、speed、space（耳障りな5つ目のS、slurping〈すすること〉は省くことにしました）を盛り込みたかったのです。sobaはもちろんそのまま。stand-and-goで、ただダラダラするわけでも、隣の人と長話をするわけでもない――人々のあわただしい様子が明確になります。spaceを表現するのは大変でした。人がぎゅう詰めになることが多いということを伝えるためにcompartmentにしようかと思ったのですが、それだと立ち食いそば屋が閉ざされた空間に思えてしまい、のれんで仕切られているとはいえ、しっくりこないと判断しました。stallなら、もっと開放的な店を思い起こさせてくれます。

丼もの

010

topped rice bowl

トッピングされた丼

 文で説明してみよう！

Donburimono are bowls of rice topped with meat, vegetables, or other ingredients.

丼物とは、ご飯の上に肉や野菜などの具材を乗せたもののこと。

 3語フレーズを会話で使おう！

My brother is so carb crazy that whenever he eats a **topped rice bowl**, he then tops that off with a separate bowl of plain rice.

私の兄は炭水化物狂で、レストランに行くといつも丼物を食べ、さらにその後、別の丼で白飯を平らげるのです。

Andrew's Point

There is such a variety of *donburimono* that I felt I had to stick with accuracy rather than invent something lest the phrase become too ambiguous or misleading. "Rice bowl" alone conveys nothing to a non-Japanese audience aside from a bowl of rice. "Topped" makes it clear that there's an additional element without imposing any limits on what that element might be. My favorite *donburimono* is *misokatsudon*. When I lived in Kyoto, there was a delivery place I called up often— perhaps too often. But when I moved to the suburbs of Nara, there was no *misokatsudon* to be found. One of these days, I'll learn how to make it myself.

丼物といっても実にいろいろあるので、曖昧な、あるいは誤解を招くような表現にならないように、へたに造語するよりも正確さにこだわるべきだと考えました。**rice bowl**だけでは、日本人以外には「丼に盛ったご飯」以上の意味を持ちません。**topped**とすれば、追加要素があることが明白になり、しかもその要素に縛りがありません。私の好きな丼物はみそカツ丼です。京都に住んでいた頃に、よく出前を頼む店がありました。でも、奈良の郊外に引っ越したら、みそカツ丼を見かけなくなりました。そのうちに、自分で作れるようになろうと思います。

うまい棒
Puffy Rod Snack 膨らんだ棒状のおやつ

Umaibō, literally translated as "delicious stick," is a small, tube-shaped, puffed corn snack made in a variety of flavors.

うまい棒は、直訳すると「おいしい棒」で、さまざまなフレーバーで作られる小さな筒状のトウモロコシ粉を膨らましたスナックである。

Few children can resist scarfing down a **Puffy Rod Snack** at snack time.

おやつの時間にうまい棒をほおばるのを我慢できる子供など、ほとんどいません。

うまみ
the fifth taste 第5の味

Umami is one of the five main categories of tastes in food, representing the savory taste triggered by glutamates.

うま味は、食品における味の5大カテゴリーの一つで、グルタミン酸によってもたらされる香ばしい味を指す。

Could there be a more satisfying source of **the fifth taste** than a quattro formaggi pizza?

クワトロ・フォルマッジ・ピザ以上に満足できるうま味の源があるでしょうか。

おせち料理
new year's fare 新年の料理

Osechiryōri is traditional cuisine served during the New Year holiday, composed of a large number of exquisitely prepared small dishes.

おせち料理は、正月休みに出される伝統料理で、絶妙に調理されたたくさんの小盛り料理で構成されている。

My family is super picky about what they eat, so I always make out like a bandit when we get **new year's fare** because there's almost nothing I don't like.

私の家族は食べるものにとてもうるさいので、おせち料理を食べるときにはいつも得をした気分になります。自分の嫌いなものはほとんど含まれていないからです。

おでん
one-pot winter-time stew 大鍋1つの冬季向けシチュー

Especially popular in the winter, *oden* is a pot of simmered savory broth filled with such things as sliced *daikon*, boiled egg, and fish cakes.

特に冬に人気のおでんは、大根の輪切り、ゆで卵、かまぼこなどが入った煮汁鍋のこと。

No matter how much **one-pot winter-time stew** Ira eats, he's always hungry again 15 minutes after he finishes.

アイラは、いくらおでんを食べても、食べ終わって15分後にはまたおなかが空いているのです。

お好み焼き
pan-fried savory pancake 焼いた香ばしいパンケーキ

Okonomiyaki is a type of savory pancake made with flour, eggs, cabbage, and a variety of toppings.

お好み焼きは、小麦粉、卵、キャベツにさまざまなトッピングを加えて作る香ばしいパンケーキの一種である。

When I visited my friend in Hiroshima and went out for dinner, I was surprised to find my **pan-fried savory pancake** resting atop a bed of *yakisoba* noodles.

広島の友人を訪ね、一緒に食事に出かけたとき、焼きそばの上にお好み焼きが乗っているのに驚きました。

かまぼこ
cured fish paste 加工処理された魚の練り物

🗒 *Kamaboko*, also known as fish cake, is a type of cured *surimi*, which is a paste made from minced fish.

かまぼこは、魚のすり身から作られる練り物の一種で、魚のケーキとも呼ばれる。

💬 It's not unusual for my kids to abandon their silverware and chopsticks only to pull the **cured fish paste** out of their *udon* and eat it with their bare hands.

うちの子供たちはしょっちゅう、フォークや箸を使わずに、素手でうどんからかまぼこを拾い出して食べています。

こんにゃく
jelly-like konjac-based food ゼリー状のコンニャク製食品

🗒 *Konnyaku* is a jelly-like food product made from processing the corm of the konjac plant.

こんにゃくは、コンニャクの球茎を加工したゼリー状の食品である。

💬 I love **jelly-like konjac-based food** when it's part of a flavorful dish, but when I once tried eating it by itself, it was pretty repulsive.

私はこんにゃくが風味豊かな料理の具材の一つとしてなら大好きですが、一度こんにゃく単体で食べてみたときにはかなりの嫌悪感を覚えました。

しゃもじ
specialized rice paddle コメ用に特化したヘラ

🗒 A *shamoji* is a flat rice paddle used for preparing, stirring, and serving rice.

しゃもじは、ご飯を準備したり、かき交ぜたり、よそったりするときに使う平らなコメ用へらである。

When Ryan visited Miyajima and saw the largest **specialized rice paddle** in the world, he couldn't help but wonder how big its accompanying rice pot must be.

ライアンは宮島を訪れ、世界最大のしゃもじを見たとき、そのしゃもじに合う釜はどれほど大きいのだろう、と考えずにはいられませんでした。

ぜんざい
mochi bean soup 餅とアズキのスープ

Zenzai is a traditional soup made with *azuki* beans and served with hot *mochi*.

ぜんざいはアズキで作った伝統的なスープで、熱い餅が入っている。

Though it's considered a dessert, **mochi bean soup** fills me up as if it were a complete meal.

デザートとはいえ、ぜんざいはまるで1食分の料理であるかのように私のおなかを満たしてくれます。

せんべい
mindblowing rice cracker 刺激的なコメのクラッカー

With a history spanning more than 1,000 years, *senbei* are rice crackers usually enjoyed as a snack.

1000年を超える歴史を持ったせんべいはコメのクラッカーで、通常、スナックとして食べられる。

While American "rice cakes" taste and feel like little more than styrofoam, **mindblowing rice crackers** are so addictive they should be illegal.

アメリカの餅は発泡スチロールのような味と感触ですが、せんべいは中毒性が強すぎるので法律で禁じるべきです。

そば湯
hot soba water 熱いそばの水

📄 *Sobayu* is the water in which *soba* was cooked, and it's often served as part of a drink after a meal of *soba*.

そば湯はそばをゆでたお湯のことで、そばを食べた後の飲み物として出されることが多い。

💬 With a range of health benefits, including smoother digestion and lower blood pressure, **hot soba water** could easily take off as a health product worldwide.

消化をスムーズにする、血圧を下げるなど、さまざまな健康効果を持つそば湯は、健康食品としてすぐに全世界に普及する可能性があります。

デコポン
sweet, seedless orange 甘い種なしオレンジ

📄 A *dekopon* is a seedless and sweet variety of Japanese mandarin orange with a naval-like protuberance at the top.

デコポンは、種がなく甘いミカンの品種で、上部にへそのような突起がある。

💬 Curiously, in the United States, **sweet, seedless oranges** are referred to as "sumos."

不思議なことに、アメリカではデコポンは「相撲」と呼ばれています。

どら焼き
red bean pancake アズキパンケーキ

📄 *Dorayaki* is a confection consisting of red bean paste sandwiched by two palm-sized, pancake-like patties.

どら焼きは、あんこを手のひらサイズのパンケーキのようなパティー2枚で挟んだお菓子である。

Sure, the limited-time-only seasonal **red bean pancake** is good, but I prefer the classic.

確かに期間限定の季節のどら焼きもおいしいけれど、私は通常品のほうが好きです。

とんかつ
deep-fried pork cutlet 揚げた豚肉のカツレツ

Tonkatsu are pork cutlets that have been breaded with *panko* and deep-fried.

トンカツとは、パン粉を付けて揚げた豚肉のカツレツのこと。

Some people may think it's weird, but whenever I go out for **deep-fried pork cutlets** and they offer all-you-can-eat shredded cabbage, I always get at least three helpings.

変だと思う人もいるかもしれませんが、トンカツを食べに行って千切りキャベツが食べ放題だと、いつも3回はお代わりしてしまうのです。

のり
dried edible seaweed 乾燥した食用海藻

Made from a type of red algae, *nori* is a dried, edible seaweed often used to wrap rolls of *sushi* or rice balls.

紅藻類の一種から作られるのりは、乾燥した食用の海藻で、巻きずしやおにぎりを包むのによく使われる。

Junko munches on so much **dried edible seaweed** while she studies that sometimes she'll go through as many as 100 sheets in a day!

ジュンコは勉強しながら大量ののりをむしゃむしゃ食べ、日に100枚も食べてしまうことがあります！

ひつまぶし
eel three ways   ウナギの3つの食べ方

Hitsumabushi is a Nagoya delicacy whereby broiled freshwater eel mixed with rice is eaten in three different ways.

ひつまぶしとは、ウナギの蒲焼きをご飯に混ぜて3つの方法で食べる名古屋の料理のこと。

A local delivery place has **eel three ways** on its menu, but ever since I visited Nagoya and tried the dish at the restaurant that claims to have invented it, delivery **eel three ways** simply doesn't cut it.

地元のデリバリーの店のメニューにひつまぶしがあるのですが、名古屋を訪れ、ひつまぶしを考案したという店で食べて以来、デリバリーのひつまぶしは食べられません。

ふりかけ
sprinkled rice seasoning   ばらまかれたご飯用調味料

Furikake is a dry condiment, often sprinkled atop rice, consisting of such ingredients as seaweed, sesame seeds, salt, egg, and fish flakes.

ふりかけは乾燥した調味料で、たいていご飯の上に振りかけられ、のり、ゴマ、塩、卵、魚のフレークなどで構成されている。

Before he learned to cook for himself properly, Andrew would often make a dinner of little more than rice and **sprinkled rice seasoning**.

自炊を覚える前、アンドリューはよく、ほぼご飯とふりかけだけの夕食を作っていました。

ポッキー
Skinny Snack Stick 細い棒状スナック菓子

Pokkī, named for the snapping sound of the onomatopoeic word "pokkiri," are a brand of sweet snack sticks first sold in the 1960s.

ポッキーは、「ポッキリ」という擬音語から名付けられた、1960年代に発売された甘い棒状スナック菓子の商標である。

Once Jonas dives into a pack of **Skinny Snack Sticks**, he can't stop eating until it's empty.

ジョナスは一度ポッキーの袋に手を入れると、空になるまで食べるのを止められません。

ゆば
dried tōfu skin 乾燥させた豆腐の皮

Yuba is the thin layer of coagulated soy proteins that forms on the surface during the production of soy milk, and it is treated as a delicacy.

ゆばとは、豆乳を作る際に表面にできる大豆タンパクの凝固した薄い膜のことで、珍味として扱われる。

While Chef Ben isn't himself a fan of plain **dried tōfu skin**, he appreciates its versatility and includes it in many of his restaurant's dishes.

シェフのベンは、自分ではプレーンなゆばが好きなわけではないのですが、その万能性を高く評価し、自分のレストランの多くの料理に取り入れています。

015

ようかん
bean paste jelly あんこゼリー

📄 *Yōkan* is a thick, jelly-like confection chiefly made from *azuki* beans, sugar, and agar-agar.

ようかんは、濃厚なゼリー状の菓子で、主にアズキ、砂糖、寒天から作られる。

💬 The young child jiggled the **bean paste jelly** softly with her fork and asked her mother innocently, "Is it still alive?"

その小さな子供はフォークでようかんを軽く揺すりながら、無邪気に母親に「まだ生きてるの？」と尋ねました。

わらび餅
jelly-like bracken confection ゼリー状のワラビのお菓子

📄 *Warabimochi* is a jelly-like confection made from bracken root starch (*warabiko*) and covered or dipped in sweet toasted soybean flour (*kinako*).

わらび餅は、ワラビの根のでんぷん（わらび粉）で作ったゼリー状の菓子で、きな粉をまぶしたり付けたりして食べる。

💬 **Jelly-like bracken confection** seems like a snack that would never go mainstream in America because it's simply not sweet or rich enough.

わらび餅はアメリカでは決して一般化しなさそうなお菓子です。ひとえに甘味やこくが足りないからです。

飴細工
meticulously hand-crafted candy
念入りに手作りしたキャンディー

Amezaiku is the traditional Japanese craft of shaping *mizuame*, a sugar syrup, into exquisite candy sculptures.

飴細工とは、水飴、つまり砂糖シロップを精巧な飴の彫刻品に成形する日本の伝統工芸品のこと。

I have a love-hate relationship with **meticulously hand-crafted candies**: I know I have to eat them eventually, but it seems like a desecration of fine art.

私は飴細工が好きでもあり嫌いでもあります。いずれは食べてしまわなければならないのは分かっているけれど、芸術を冒涜しているように感じるからです。

わさび
spicy green paste 辛い緑のペースト

Wasabi refers to both Japanese horseradish, a plant of the mustard family (Brassicaceae), and the pungent green paste into which it's often made.

わさびは、アブラナ科の植物であるワサビと、たいていそれを元にして作る辛味のある緑色のペーストの両方を指す。

The stinging that pervaded my mouth was one thing; when I wiped the tears from my eyes with fingers coated in **spicy green paste** residue, that's when I entered a whole new dimension of pain.

口の中全体にしみわたる刺すような辛さも強烈でしたが、わさびの残りが付いた指で目から涙をぬぐったとき、私はまったく新しい次元の痛みに襲われました。

かつお節
shaved dried skipjack 削られた乾燥カツオ

📄 *Katsuobushi* is dried, smoked skipjack tuna, frequently used in Japanese cuisine to add a rich *umami* flavor.

かつお節はカツオを乾燥させて燻製にしたもので、日本料理で濃厚なうま味を加えるためによく使われる。

💬 When **shaved dried skipjack** dances atop my *okonomiyaki*, it's like dinner and a show.

お好み焼きの上でかつお節が踊ると、まるでディナーショーのようです。

義理チョコ
obligatory Valentine's chocolate
義務的なバレンタインのチョコレート

📄 *Girichoko*, or "obligation chocolate," is chocolate given by women to male coworkers and acquaintances on Valentine's Day as a customary gift.

義理チョコとはつまり「義務的なチョコレート」で、バレンタインデーに女性が男性の同僚や知人に贈るチョコレートのこと。

💬 While I do enjoy my **obligatory Valentine's chocolate** bounty, on White Day I'm forced to wonder whether it's really worth it.

私は義理チョコを贈られれば喜んで受け取りますが、一方で、ホワイトデーには、本当にその価値があるのかどうか考えざるを得なくなります。

菜箸
extra-long cooking chopsticks 並外れて長い調理用箸

📄 *Saibashi* are elongated, sturdy chopsticks used for cooking.

菜箸は細長くて丈夫な箸で、調理に使われる。

💬 Whenever I cook with **extra-long cooking chopsticks**, I always end up dropping things and making a mess, so I tend to use regular-sized chopsticks instead.

菜箸を使って料理をすると、いつも食材を落として散らかしてしまうので、私はどちらかというと普通の長さの箸のほうを使います。

七味唐辛子
pepper-based spice mix トウガラシベースの混合香辛料

📄 *Shichimitōgarashi* is a unique blend of spices typically made from red chilis, *sanshō* pepper, hemp or poppy seeds, sesame seeds, ground ginger, *yuzu* or mandarin orange peel, and *nori*.

七味唐辛子は香辛料のユニークなブレンドで、通常、赤トウガラシ、サンショウ、アサの実またはケシの実、ゴマ、刻んだショウガ、ユズまたはミカンの皮、のりで作られる。

💬 Food flavored with **pepper-based spice mix** isn't so much hot as it is tingly, thanks to the *sanshō* pepper.

七味唐辛子で風味付けされた料理は、サンショウのおかげで辛いというよりもピリピリします。

酒
alcoholic rice brew コメの醸造酒

📄 *Sake* is an alcoholic beverage made from fermented rice.

酒は、発酵させたコメで作ったアルコール飲料である。

💬 No matter how many times I correct my American friends, they still refer to **alcoholic rice brew** as "SAH-kee."

アメリカ人の友人たちは、何度訂正してもいまだに酒のことを「サキー」と発音します。

焼酎
Japanese hard liquor 日本の強い酒

Shōchū, literally translated as "burnt liquor," is a type of hard alcohol distilled from rice, barley, sweet potatoes, buckwheat, or brown sugar.

焼酎は、直訳すると「焼けた酒」で、コメ、麦、サツマイモ、ソバの実、黒砂糖などから蒸留される強い酒の一種である。

When my coworkers and I go out after a long day, we usually toast over beer before moving on to **Japanese hard liquor**.

同僚と長い一日を終えて街に繰り出すと、たいていビールで乾杯してから焼酎に移ります。

焼き鳥
grilled chicken skewer 網焼き鶏肉串

Yakitori, literally translated as "grilled chicken," are skewers of bite-sized pieces of grilled meat from various parts of a chicken.

焼き鳥とは、直訳すれば「網焼きした鶏肉」で、鶏肉のさまざまな部位を一口大に切って串刺しにして焼いたもののこと。

Outside Japan, there is no Japanese food more well-known than *sushi*, so visitors to the country are often surprised to find that **grilled chicken skewers** are so common.

日本以外では、すしほど有名な和食はないので、日本を訪れた外国人はたいてい、焼き鳥がとても一般的であることに驚きます。

食パン
pillowy breakfast bread 枕のような朝食向けパン

Shokupan, literally translated as "food bread" or "eating bread," is the king of loaves, pillowy and white, gracing breakfast tables across Japan.

食パンとは、直訳すれば「食品パン」または「食べるパン」であり、枕のように柔らかく白い、パンの王者として、日本中の朝食の食卓を飾っている。

When her dog ripped her pillow to shreds, Annie briefly considered stuffing a few loaves of **pillowy breakfast bread** into a pillowcase as a substitute.

愛犬に枕をズタズタにされたアニーは、枕カバーに食パンを数斤詰めて代用することを一瞬、考えました。

食品サンプル
realistic food model リアルな食品模型

Shokuhin sampuru, literally translated as "food samples," are realistic food models found in the windows of many restaurants and the display cases of many other food purveyors to give customers a clear indication of what to expect.

食品サンプルは、直訳すると「食べ物の見本」で、多くのレストランのショーウィンドーや食料品店の陳列ケースに見られるリアルな食品の模型である。

I swear that if you put the *gyōza* at the joint down the street right next to its **realistic food model** in their window, I couldn't tell them apart.

この通り沿いの店の餃子を、その店の陳列ウインドーの中の食品サンプルの餃子を並べてみても、絶対に見分けがつきません。

生菓子
artistic confectionery creation
芸術的な菓子創作物

018

Namagashi, literally translated as "raw sweets," are a type of Japanese confection made of rice flour and sweet bean paste, formed into shapes both elaborate and delicate to reflect the season.

生菓子とは、直訳すれば「生の菓子」であり、米粉とあんこで作られる和菓子の一種である。丹精込めて絶妙な形に作り込み、季節を反映させる。

The **artistic confectionery creations** I was presented with at the tea ceremony looked too beautiful to eat, but I knew I would cause offense were I to refuse that.

茶の湯で出された生菓子は、食べるにはあまりにも美しすぎましたが、断れば角が立つことは分かっていました。

精進料理
Buddhist vegetarian cuisine 仏教徒の菜食主義料理

Shōjin ryōri is a traditional cuisine deeply rooted in Buddhist principles that is not only made without any meat or fish products but also eschews strong flavors altogether.

精進料理は仏教の教えに深く根ざした伝統料理で、肉や魚介類をいっさい使わないだけでなく、決して濃い味付けをしない。

The simplicity of **Buddhist vegetarian cuisine** belies its sophistication: it is a transcendent feast for all of one's senses.

精進料理は、その洗練された味わいとは裏腹にシンプルで、あらゆる感覚に作用する超越的なごちそうです。

煎茶
steamed green tea 煎じた緑茶

Sencha is green tea made by steeping processed whole leaves of the small-leaf Camellia sinesis in hot water.

煎茶は、小葉ツバキの全葉を加工し、湯に浸して出した緑茶である。

Although the health benefits of **steamed green tea** are many, if you incorporate an expensive variety like *gyokuro* into your daily routine, you will certainly pay for it.

煎茶には健康上の利点が少なくありませんが、玉露のような高価な品種を日常的にたしなむと、それなりにお金がかかります。

緑茶
green tea, all-inclusive 総称としての緑茶

Ryokucha is the umbrella term for green tea, which includes *sencha*, the most common, as well as *matcha*, *hōjicha*, *gyokuro*, and *bancha*.

緑茶とは、最も一般的な煎茶をはじめ、抹茶、ほうじ茶、玉露、番茶などを含むお茶の総称である。

When Dave finally returned to Canada after a decade in Japan, he was thrilled to find **green tea, all-inclusive** at his local supermarket.

デーブは、10年間の日本滞在を終えてようやくカナダに戻ってから、近所のスーパーマーケットで緑茶を見つけて感激しました。

団子
rice flour dumpling 米粉練り物

Dango are sweet Japanese dumplings made from rice flour that come in a variety of flavors, including red bean paste, green tea, and soy sauce.

だんごは米粉でできた甘い日本の練り物で、あんや抹茶、しょうゆなどさまざまな味付けがある。

The only problem with **rice flour dumplings** is that I can never get my fill from a single stick.

だんごの唯一の問題は、1本では決して満腹にならないことです。

酎ハイ
burned liquor highball 焼けた酒のハイボール

Chūhai, a portmanteau of "shōchū" (a type of liquor) and "highball," is a distilled beverage that comes in a variety of flavors, including grapefruit, apple, peach, and cream soda.

酎ハイは、「焼酎」と「ハイボール」の合成語で、グレープフルーツ、アップル、ピーチ、クリームソーダなど、さまざまなフレーバーがある蒸留酒。

With their classes done for the week, the university students gathered by the river and cracked open some cold **burned liquor highballs** to relax.

1週間の授業が終わり、大学生たちは河原に集まって、冷たい酎ハイを開けながらくつろぎました。

漬物
Japanese preserved vegetable 和風保存野菜

Tsukemono are pickles made from vegetables that have been preserved in salt, brine, or a bed of rice bran.

漬物とは、野菜を塩、濃い塩水、またはぬか床に漬けたもの。

I was excited the first time I discovered a **Japanese preserved vegetable** specialty shop, so I bought five bags of it, but after eating them every night for a week, I started to have serious regrets.

漬物専門店を初めて発見したときには興奮して5袋も買ってしまいましたが、1週間にわたって毎晩食べ続けたあげく、真剣に後悔し始めました。

唐揚げ
flour-coated deep-fried meat 小麦粉で覆われた揚げ肉

Karaage is a Japanese cooking technique in which food—usually chicken—is coated with flour, potato starch, or corn starch and fried in cooking oil.

から揚げは、食材――通常は鶏肉――に小麦粉、片栗粉またはコーンスターチをまぶして、サラダ油で揚げる日本の調理法である。

My second-oldest son will only eat the soy sauce-flavored **flour-coated deep-fried meat** from the supermarket down the street.

私の次男は、通り沿いのスーパーマーケットで売られているしょうゆ味の唐揚げしか食べません。

豆腐
soy bean curd 大豆の凝固物

Tōfu is a food product made by coagulating soy milk and then pressing the resulting curds into solid blocks.

豆腐は豆乳を凝固させ、できた凝乳を圧力をかけて固形にした食品である。

Even though Aki has lived in America for more than fifteen years, she still anguishes over the fact that it's so difficult to find **soy bean curd** as silky and smooth as it is back in Japan.

アキはアメリカに15年以上住んでいますが、いまだに悩んでいます。日本のものほど絹のように滑らかな豆腐がなかなか見つからないからです。

鍋
hot pot cuisine 火鍋料理

Nabe, a winter staple, is a type of hot pot dish packed with ingredients that include meat, fish, and vegetables.

鍋は冬の定番の食べ物で、肉、魚、野菜などの具がたっぷり入った火鍋料理の一種である。

Had I known noodles would arrive at the end of the **hot pot cuisine**, I wouldn't have stuffed my face with so much meat and vegetables.

鍋の最後に麺が出されると知っていたら、あんなに肉や野菜をおなかに詰め込まなかったでしょう。

納豆
fermented stinky beans 発酵した臭い豆

Nattō is a slimy, sticky, stringy, smelly dish consisting of soybeans that have been fermented with Bacillus subtilis bacteria.

納豆はヌルヌル、ネバネバして糸を引く臭い食べ物で、大豆を枯草菌で発酵させたものである。

No matter how much I tried to mask the taste of **fermented stinky beans** with soy sauce, eggs, mustard, and anything else I could find in my kitchen, it still made me a little queasy.

しょうゆ、卵、マスタード、その他台所にあるものでいくら納豆の味をごまかそうとしても、やはり少し気分が悪くなってしまいました。

梅干し
pickled Japanese plums 酢漬けの日本のプラム

Both salty and sour, *umeboshi* are brined Japanese plums.

塩気と酸味を併せ持つ梅干しは、日本の梅を塩漬けにしたものである。

None of Hideki's four children eat the **pickled Japanese plums** that come with their delivery *bentō*, so Hideki always ends up with a handful.

ヒデキの４人の子供たちの誰も、デリバリーの弁当に付いてくる梅干しを食べないので、ヒデキはいつも困ってしまいます。

明太子
salted pollock roe 塩漬けのタラの卵

Mentaiko is pollock roe, or the roe that has been marinated with red chili peppers and other spices.

明太子とは、スケトウダラの卵のこと、あるいはそれを赤トウガラシやその他の香辛料で漬け込んだもののことである。

I myself find **salted pollock roe** delicious, but why there's a chain of theme parks dedicated to the delicacy is totally bewildering.

私自身は明太子をおいしいと思いますが、なぜ明太子専門のテーマパークのチェーンがあるのか、まったく理解できません。

餅
glutinous rice cake 粘着質のコメケーキ

Mochi is a type of rice cake made of sweet glutinous rice flour called *mochigome*.

餅はケーキの一種で、餅米と呼ばれる甘く弾力のあるコメの粉でできている。

Even before moving to Japan in the early 2000s, I knew of **glutinous rice cake** because I frequently bought **glutinous rice cake** ice cream from the Trader Joe's market down the street from my apartment.

2000年代初頭に日本に引っ越してくる前から、私は餅を知っていました。自宅アパートがあった通り沿いのトレーダージョーズというマーケットで頻繁に餅アイスクリームを買っていたからです。

馬刺し
raw horse meat 生の馬肉

Basashi is thinly sliced horse meat that is consumed cold and raw, often with condiments such as sliced onions, grated ginger, and garlic.

馬刺しは馬肉を薄くスライスしたもので、冷やして生で食べ、たいていスライスしたタマネギ、おろしたショウガ、ニンニクなどの薬味を添える。

The prospect of **raw horse meat** being served in America is nil, not only because most Americans find the thought unpalatable, but also because the USDA does not have a budget for horse meat inspection.

アメリカで馬刺しが提供される見込みがほぼないのは、ほとんどのアメリカ人が口に合わないと考えることに加えて、米国農務省が馬肉検査の予算を計上していないからです。

油揚げ
twice-fried tōfu pouches 2度揚げた豆腐の小袋

Abura-age is a type of Japanese deep-fried *tōfu* that is made by cutting *tōfu* into slices and deep-frying it two times.

油揚げとは、油で揚げた日本の豆腐の一種で、豆腐を薄く切って二度揚げしたもの。

Without **twice-fried tōfu pouches**, my *udon* feels like it has lost part of its soul.

油揚げがないと、私は自分のうどんが魂の一部を失ったように感じるのです。

まんじゅう
bean paste confection あんこ菓子

Manjū is a steamed, flour-based pastry stuffed with red bean paste.

まんじゅうは小麦粉をベースにした蒸し菓子で、あんこが詰まっている。

The doctor told me I needed to lose weight, but when I saw a streetwise vendor selling **bean paste confection** on my way home, I couldn't help but pop one into my mouth.

医者からはやせたほうがいいと言われたのですが、帰り道でまんじゅうを売っている露天を見て、たまらず1つ口に入れてしまいました。

大福
mochi with filling 中身を詰めた餅

Daifuku is a confection consisting of a small round *mochi* with a sweet filling, such as red bean paste.

大福とは、小さな丸い餅にあんこのような甘い中身を詰めた菓子のこと。

The outrageous prices of the **mochi with filling** shop that opened in my neck of suburbia were sure to result in swift bankruptcy, but after a year in business, I was surprised to see no signs of financial distress.

私の住む郊外にオープンした大福の店は、その法外な価格設定からすぐにつぶれるにちがいないと思われたのですが、1年間営業して経営難に陥る様子も見られず、驚きました。

立ち飲み
casual standing bar 気軽に立ったまま飲めるバー

Tachinomi, literally translated as "stand and drink," are small, casual, and affordable drinking establishments where there are generally no seats.

立ち飲みは、直訳すると「立って飲む」ことで、一般的に椅子がない、小さくてカジュアルな、手頃な価格の飲み屋である。

The **casual standing bars** of yore tended to be minimalist affairs, but today, I can find a chic spot by my office offering up organic French wine and resplendent charcuterie.

昔の立ち飲みは最低限のものしか置いていませんでしたが、今では、私の職場近くなどで、オーガニックのフランスワインや華やかなシャルキュトリーを提供するシックな店を見つけることができます。

Chapter
2

Custom/Tradition
習慣・伝統

おみくじ

sacred fortune slip

神聖な運勢伝票

 文で説明してみよう！

Omikuji, literally translated as "sacred lots," are fortunes printed on strips of paper available for a small fee at Shintō shrines and Buddhist temples in Japan.

おみくじとは、直訳すれば「聖なるくじ」で、日本の神社や仏閣で少額の料金で手に入る、運勢が印刷された短冊のことである。

 ３語フレーズを会話で使おう！

My friends and I got **sacred fortune slips** when we visited a shrine, so when they all revealed that they got *kyō*, I thought it best to surreptitiously slip my *dai-kichi* into my pocket .

友人たちと神社にお参りに行ったとき、私たちはおみくじを引いたのですが、友人たちが凶を引いたことが分かったので、私は自分の大吉をこっそりポケットに入れました。

Andrew's Point

When you go to a Chinese restaurant in the U.S.—and, I'm told, much of the West—you can expect to receive a fortune cookie: a crisp, sugary wafer with a short, written fortune in it. (Interestingly, fortune cookies actually originated in Kyoto, according to a *New York Times* article.) To differentiate from this type of fortune and convey the somewhat more religious significance, I added "sacred." I always liked that even with a bad fortune, you could cause it to "slip" away by tying it to a tree branch or wire fence. Of course, the "slip" here refers to a paper "slip," however.

アメリカで——それに、聞いた話では西洋の多くの場所で——中華料理店に行くと、フォーチュンクッキーをもらえます（興味深いことに、『ニューヨークタイムズ』の記事によると、実はフォーチュンクッキーの発祥地は京都だそうです）。この種の運勢と区別し、宗教的な意味を伝えるために、sacred を付け加えました。悪い運勢が出ても、木の枝や金網にくくりつけて「追いやる（slip）」ことができるところを、私は常々気に入っているのです。もちろん、ここで言う slip とは紙の「伝票」のことですが。

見合い

023

arranged matchmaking meeting

あつらえられた結婚仲介の会合

 文で説明してみよう！

Miai is a type of matchmaking whereby a woman and man are formally introduced to each other as potential marriage partners.

見合いとは、女性と男性を将来の結婚相手として正式に紹介し合うことである。

 3語フレーズを会話で使おう！

Nowadays, people are more likely to find a life partner online than through traditional **arranged matchmaking meetings**, but the practice is not yet uncommon.

今日では、従来の見合いよりもネットで人生のパートナーを見つけることのほうが多くなっていますが、まだお見合いが珍しくなったというほどでもありません。

Andrew's Point

I had to be careful with this term to avoid potential confusion with similar terms. The term "arranged marriage" brings to mind cultures that make agreements without much regard for individual choice or emotional connection. In some cases, couples don't meet face to face until their wedding day (this is becoming less common globally for a variety of reasons). I also wanted to make a distinction from Western "matchmaking." While similar to "miai," Western matchmaking often emphasizes personal interests and romantic compatibility, and may not involve families to the same extent. That's why I modified it by adding the word "meeting."

似たような言葉との混同を避けるために、この言葉には注意しなければなりませんでした。arranged marriageと言うと、個人の選択や感情的なつながりをあまり考慮せずに取り決めをする文化が思い浮かびます。場合によっては、結婚式の日までカップルが顔を合わせないこともあります（さまざまな理由から、これは世界的にあまり一般的ではなくなってきています）。また、欧米のmatchmakingとは一線を画したいと思いました。「見合い」と似ていますが、欧米のmatchmakingは個人の趣味や恋愛の相性が重視されることが多く、家族があまり関与しないこともあります。そういうわけで、meeting という単語を加えて調整しました。

お守り

good luck talisman
幸運の護符

文で説明してみよう！

Omamori are Japanese amulets sold at Shintō shrines and Buddhist temples that confer various forms of luck or protection.

お守りは神社や仏閣で売られている日本の魔よけで、さまざまな幸運や守護を授けてくれる。

３語フレーズを会話で使おう！

Even though Mariko studied more than anyone I know, she attributed passing the entrance exam to her academic achievement **good luck talisman**.

マリコは、私が知る誰よりも勉強していたにもかかわらず、入試に合格したのは学業成就のお守りのおかげだと言っていました。

Andrew's Point

Many people all over the world have some sort of a "good luck charm." This phrase is common in English. Some people collect and carry around four-leaf clovers, some hang horseshoes in their homes, and some even keep rabbits' feet. But these items don't tend to have any religious significance. I decided that rather than "charm," "amulet" or "talisman" was more appropriate. I tend to associate "amulet" with magical powers and fantasy worlds, so "talisman" made the most sense to me. For a long time, I carried around an *omamori* in my backpack until someone told me that I was supposed to burn it at the end of the year. No one had ever told me, so it was long overdue!

世界中の多くの人が何らかの good luck charm を持っています。この言葉は英語でよく使われます。四つ葉のクローバーを集めて持ち歩く人もいれば、蹄鉄を家につるす人もいれば、ウサギの足を保管する人さえいます。しかし、これらのアイテムには宗教的な意味はありません。私は charm よりも amulet や talisman のほうが適切だと考えました。amulet と言うと、不思議な力やファンタジーの世界を連想しがちなので、talisman が一番しっくりきました。長い間、お守りをリュックに入れて持ち歩いていたところ、ある人に、お守りは年末に燃やすものだと言われました。それまで誰も教えてくれなかったので、ずいぶん遅くなってしまいました！

もみじ狩り

autumn leaf peeping

紅葉見物

文で説明してみよう！

Momijigari, literally translated as "autumn leaf hunting," is the autumn tradition of visiting areas where the leaves are changing colors.

もみじ狩りとは、直訳すれば「紅葉見物」で、紅葉の名所を巡る秋の風物詩である。

３語フレーズを会話で使おう！

One of the few silver linings of the coronavirus pandemic was that the prime spots for **autumn leaf peeping** were not jam-packed with tourists.

コロナウイルスの大流行がもたらした数少ない明るい側面の一つは、もみじ狩りの絶好のスポットが観光客でごった返さなくなったことでした。

Andrew's Point

I was set to publish this term as "autumn foliage hunting" when I heard a report on the radio about "leaf peepers." I had never heard of this term, so I looked it up and found that it's becoming more common in the northeastern region of the U.S. If you're not familiar, the leaves there are beautiful in the fall—possibly even rivaling Japan! You should come and judge for yourself. Anyway, "leaf peeper" is generally used in one of two ways: it's used as a term of appreciation from businesses that benefit from the millions of tourists, and it's used as a term of disdain from locals who have to deal with the traffic of the "foliage tours."

この言葉をautumn foliage huntingと表現しようと思っていたところ、ラジオでleaf peeper（紅葉見物客）についての報道を聞きました。それまで聞いたことのない言葉だったので調べてみると、アメリカ北東部では一般的になりつつあるとのこと。ご存じないかもしれませんが、その地域の秋の紅葉は日本に匹敵するほど美しいのです！ ぜひ、ご自分の目で確かめてみてください。とにかく、leaf peeperは一般的に2つのうちのどちらかの意味合いで使われます。一つは何百万人もの観光客から利益を得ている企業からの感謝の言葉として、もう一つは紅葉ツアーの人出に対処しなければならない地元民からの軽蔑の言葉としてです。

花見

026

cherry blossom reveling

桜の花の宴

 文で説明してみよう！

Hanami is the traditional custom of enjoying the beauty of cherry blossoms, often with friends or coworkers in a park atop large blue tarps covered with an array of food and drinks.

花見とは桜の美しさを楽しむ伝統的な習慣のことで、多くの場合、友人や同僚と一緒に、公園で大きなブルーシートの上に食べ物や飲み物を並べる。

 ３語フレーズを会話で使おう！

During **cherry blossom reveling** season, we used to get up at the crack of dawn to put down a blue tarp at one of the most well-known parks in the prefecture until we discovered a local park full of cherry blossoms and practically devoid of people.

花見のシーズンには、うちでは県内で最も有名な公園の一つにブルーシートを敷くために夜明けに起きていたのですが、そのうち桜が満開でほとんど人のいない地元の公園を発見しました。

Andrew's Point

There's the BBQ, there's the beer, there's the blue tarps, there's the unfortunate soul who has to wake up at the crack of dawn in the oftentimes frigid late-March morning, there's the laughter and the singing, there's the games, there's the rice balls and the *bentōs*, there's the soft glow of paper lanterns as the day comes to a close, and there's the shared awe as everyone looks up to admire the transient beauty of cherry blossoms in full bloom. The term "hanami" evokes so many images and so much nostalgia. But at its heart, it's a party that pays homage to cherry blossoms.

バーベキューあり、ビールあり、ブルーシートあり、3月下旬の何かと肌寒い朝、夜明けとともに起きなければならない不幸な人々あり、笑いあり、歌あり、ゲームあり、おにぎりや弁当、ちょうちんの柔らかな光に包まれながら一日が終わりを告げ、満開の桜のはかない美しさに目を見張り、畏敬の念を分かち合う。花見という言葉は、さまざまなイメージや郷愁を呼び起こします。しかしその本質は、桜に敬意を表する宴なのです。

香典

funeral condolence money

葬儀お悔やみ金

 文で説明してみよう！

Kōden is a monetary condolence gift offered to both the deceased and the bereaved at a funeral.

香典とは、葬儀の際に故人と遺族の双方に向けて贈るお悔やみの印としての金銭のこと。

 ３語フレーズを会話で使おう！

Joyce was surprised to receive a gift in exchange for the **funeral condolence money** she offered at her old Japanese teacher's funeral.

ジョイスは、日本人の恩師の葬儀で渡した香典にお返しが届いたので、驚きました。

Andrew's Point

I often conduct seminars about cross-cultural communication, and we spend a lot of time talking about what's *atarimae* among different cultures. In the U.S., giving flowers to the bereaved to offer your condolences is appropriate. Sometimes, you might bake or bring food for a family after the funeral is over so they don't have to concern themselves with such mundane matters. You can even make a donation to a charity in the name of the deceased. But directly giving a grieving American family money is unusual and sometimes inappropriate. By the way, there's an adjectival form of funeral: "funerary." However, I feel it's most often used in museums (e.g., funerary art, funerary statues) and in association with certain rituals. We wouldn't ever say "funerary flowers" or "funerary baked goods" or anything like that.

私はよく異文化コミュニケーションに関するセミナーで話し、異文化間では何が「当たり前」なのかという話に多くの時間を費やします。アメリカでは、遺族にお悔やみの花を贈るのが適切です。葬儀が終わった後、遺族が日常にわずらわされずにすむよう、食べ物を作って持って行くこともあります。故人の名前で慈善団体に寄付をすることもできます。しかし、悲嘆に暮れるアメリカ人遺族に直接お金を渡すのは異例であり、時には不適切です。ところで、funeral の形容詞形に funerary があります。しかし、これは美術館(例えば、funerary art や funerary statues のように)や特定の儀式に関連して使われることが多いように感じます。funerary flower や funerary baked goods のようには使わないのです。

初詣

year's first worship

年の最初の参拝

文で説明してみよう！

Hatsumōde is the traditional first visit of the year to a Buddhist temple or Shintō shrine to pray for a good year ahead.

初詣とは伝統的に、この先1年間の無事を祈願するために仏教寺院や神社を年初に訪れること。

3語フレーズを会話で使おう！

Because Masahiro was sent overseas for more than half a year, he didn't get to do his **year's first worship** at his hometown shrine until the middle of summer.

マサヒロは半年以上海外に派遣されていたので、地元の神社に初詣したのは真夏になってからでした。

Andrew's Point

One of the things I appreciate about religion in Japan is that it's not particularly rigid. Some years, I've done *hatsumōde* right at the stroke of midnight on New Year's Day, and other years, it's been a few days later. In 2017, I didn't pay respects at a shrine until I returned from getting my graduate degree at Harvard in late May. I visited almost halfway through the year, and there was no Judeo-Christian god ready to smite me for some unforgivable sin. Religion in Japan is flexible and accommodating. I can make my first annual worship in my own time, giving me a meaningful moment for spiritual reflection.

日本の宗教について私が評価していることの一つは、特段、厳格なものではないという点です。元日の午前零時ちょうどに初詣をした年もあれば、数日後に詣でた年もあります。2017年は、5月下旬にハーバード大学の大学院で学位を取得して帰日するまで、神社に詣でませんでした。1年のほぼ半ばになってから訪れたのに、ユダヤ教やキリスト教の神のように、私が許されざる罪を犯したとして叱責する神はいませんでした。日本の宗教は柔軟で融通が利きます。私は自分の好きなタイミングで初詣ができ、有意義に内省する時間を過ごせるのです。

正座

formal floor sitting

正式な床着座

文で説明してみよう！

Seiza is a formal way of sitting whereby one folds one's legs under one's thighs, resting one's posterior on one's heels.

正座は正式な座り方のことで、両脚を太ももの下に折り畳み、尻をかかとの上に乗せる。

3語フレーズを会話で使おう！

The austerity of the ceremony demanded a hush that was broken when Missy cried out, "pins and needles!" as the **formal floor sitting** had proved too much for her legs to bear.

その儀式は厳粛で静寂が求められる場でしたが、ミッシーが「脚がしびれた！」と叫んだので、その静寂が破られてしまいました。正座は彼女の脚には耐えられなかったのです。

Andrew's Point

I find it curious that I no longer feel pins and needles in my legs when sitting *seiza* for long periods of time. I don't go as far as my mother-in-law, though, who will sit *seiza* style in a chair at the dining room table. I don't know how or why she does that. But I guess I got used to doing it on *tatami*, anyway. It's rare to see someone sitting *seiza* style on the floor in the West. And there's no Western association between *seiza* and formality. Perhaps these days, some people draw an association between *seiza* and *Zen* Buddhism, however.

長時間、正座していても脚がしびれなくなったのは不思議です。とはいえ、義母のようなわけにはいきません。彼女はダイニングルームのテーブル脇の椅子に正座するのですから。どのように、あるいはなぜそうするのかは分かりません。でも、とにかく私は畳の上で正座することに慣れてしまったのでしょう。欧米で床に正座している人を見ることはめったにありません。また、欧米では正座と格式を結びつけることもありません。最近では、正座と禅を結びつけて考える人はいるのかもしれませんが。

地蔵

030

child guardian statue

子供守護像

文で説明してみよう！

Jizō are small stone statues often dressed in a red knitted bib and cap, modeled after the image of *Jizō Bosatsu*, the guardian deity of children and travelers.

地蔵は小さな石像で、赤い糸で編んだよだれ掛けと帽子をかぶっていることが多く、子供や旅人の守り神である地蔵菩薩を模している。

３語フレーズを会話で使おう！

Something compels me to offer a slight bow whenever I'm hiking and come across a **child guardian statue**.

ハイキングをしていてお地蔵さんに出くわすと、つい軽くおじぎをしてしまいます。

Andrew's Point

There's a scene in *My Neighbor Totoro* where the young girls Satsuki and Mei take refuge from the rain in a small shelter housing a lone *jizō* while they wait for the storm to subside. The primary purpose of *jizō* is to serve as the guardian of children, so there's no better place for them to wait than beside the small statue. My kids enjoy the siblings' exchange with Satsuki's classmate Kanta, who offers them an umbrella, but I enjoy the imagery. I've always had a fondness for *jizō*, and I cannot help but to offer a bow to them whenever I cross by one. Before my kids were born, I ran and hiked a lot, so I did a lot of bowing.

『となりのトトロ』に、少女サツキとメイが雨宿りをするシーンがあります。小さな地蔵堂の中で嵐が去るのを待つのです。地蔵の主な目的は子供を守ることですから、この小さな像のそばほど、待つのにうってつけの場所はありません。私の子供たちは、サツキの同級生で傘を差し出してくれるカンタと姉妹のやりとりが好きですが、私はこの地蔵の比喩的な描写を楽しんでいます。私は昔から地蔵が好きで、地蔵の前を通りかかるたびにおじぎをせずにはいられません。子供が生まれる前、よくランニングやハイキングをしていたので、頻繁におじぎしていました。

忘年会

end-of-year drinking party
年末の飲み会

 文で説明してみよう！

A *bōnenkai* is a drinking party usually held among friends or coworkers to shrug off the stresses of the year and start the coming year anew.

忘年会とは、通常、友人や同僚の間で開かれる飲み会のことで、その年のストレスを解消し、新たな年を迎えるために行われる。

 3語フレーズを会話で使おう！

As COVID-19 rendered in-person gatherings infeasible, we had no choice but to hold our office's **end-of-year drinking party** on Zoom.

新型コロナウイルス感染症のせいで直接顔を合わせることが難しくなったため、私たちの職場ではZoomで忘年会を開くしかありませんでした。

Andrew's Point

I wanted to call this three-word term "forget-the-year drinking party," but that unfortunately gives no indication of when a *bōnenkai* actually takes place. One could just as easily forget the previous year at a *shinnenkai*, making the term confusing. So "end-of-year" was a must. But, whether or not you drink alcohol, I think most people would agree that it's traditionally considered a night to get sloshed, so "drinking party" is apt. For some reason, while I have vivid memories of my first few years living Japan, I can't remember my first few *bōnenkai*. Perhaps, for me, they should be called "forget-the-party drinking party."

私はこの3語フレーズを **forget-the-year drinking party** としたかったのですが、残念ながらそれでは忘年会が実際にいつ行われるのかが分かりません。新年会で前年を忘れることも簡単にできてしまうので、この表現では紛らわしいのです。だから **end-of-year** が必須でした。でも、お酒を飲む飲まないにかかわらず、忘年会は昔から酔っ払いの夜と見なされているので、**drinking party** がふさわしいというのは衆目の一致するところだと思います。どういうわけか、日本に住み始めてからの数年間のことは鮮明に覚えているのに、最初の頃の忘年会の記憶がありません。たぶん、私にとっては、**forget-the-party drinking party** と呼ぶべきものなのかもしれません。

エイサー
Okinawan folk dance 沖縄の民族舞踊

032

📄 ***Eisā*** is a type of Okinawan folk dance performed with *taiko* drums and the *sanshin*, Okinawa's traditional three-stringed instrument.

エイサーは沖縄の民族舞踊の一種で、太鼓と三線という沖縄の伝統的な三弦楽器で踊る。

💬 Unlike traditional **Okinawan folk dance**, a modern form of it called "club team Eisā" admits anyone into their dance groups regardless of their heritage.

伝統的なエイサーとは異なり、「クラブ・チーム・エイサー」と呼ばれる現代的なエイサーは、伝統に関係なく誰でもダンスグループに参加できます。

大掃除
deep household cleaning 念入りな家庭内掃除

📄 ***Ōsōji***, literally translated as "big cleaning," is a major household cleaning event akin to "spring cleaning" in the U.S. that takes place right before the new year.

大掃除は、直訳すると「大きな掃除」で、アメリカの「春の清掃」のような大掛かりな家庭内の掃除が、新年を迎える直前に行われる。

💬 During my family's **deep household cleaning**, I apologized to my brother when I found the baseball glove I had accused him of stealing earlier in the year.

わが家で大掃除をしている最中、私は弟に謝りました。その年の前半に弟が盗んだものと決めつけてしまった野球のグラブが出てきたからです。

おしぼり
mealtime wet towel 食事時の濡れタオル

Oshibori are small, wet towels offered to customers for wiping their hands in restaurants, bars, hotels, and even some airplanes.

おしぼりは小さな濡れタオルで、レストランやバー、ホテル、一部の飛行機内で、手をふくために客に提供される。

When Gloria saw all the passengers on the airplane wiping their faces with their **mealtime wet towel**, she thought, "When in Rome!" and discarded etiquette in favor of mopping her brow.

グロリアは、飛行機の中で乗客全員がおしぼりで顔をふいているのを見て、「郷に入れば郷に従え！」と思い、エチケットを忘れて額をふきました。

お宮参り
newborn shrine visit 新生児の神社参拝

Omiyamairi, literally translated as "shrine visit," is a traditional Shintō rite of passage whereby approximately one month after a birth, parents—and often grandparents, too—take their baby to a Shintō shrine where a priest will pray for the baby's health and happiness.

お宮参りとは、直訳すると「神社参拝」で、神道の伝統的な通過儀礼の一つである。出産から約1カ月後、両親——そして多くの場合、祖父母も——が赤ん坊を連れて神社に赴き、神職にその子の健康と幸せを願う祈祷をしてもらう。

Kanako was so proud when her baby was the only one of six that didn't cry at the **newborn shrine visit** ceremony.

カナコがとても誇らしげだったのは、お宮参りのとき、6人の赤ん坊の中で泣かなかったのは自分の子供だけだったからです。

033

お中元
mid-year appreciation gift
年の半ばの感謝贈答品

Ochūgen are customary mid-year gifts bestowed upon those to whom a person feels indebted.

お中元とは、世話になった人へ向けた年の半ばの習慣的な贈答品のことである。

Shirley's biggest client gave her the most expensive melon she had ever seen as a **mid-year appreciation gift**.

シャーリーの一番の顧客は、彼女が見たこともないような最高級メロンをお中元に贈ってきました。

お歳暮
end-of-year appreciation gift 年末の感謝贈答品

Oseibo are customary end-of-year gifts bestowed upon those to whom a person feels indebted.

お歳暮とは、世話になった人へ向けた年末の習慣的な贈答品のことである。

I was surprised to receive a slab of smoked horse meat as an **end-of-year appreciation gift**, but it was unbelievably delicious.

馬肉の燻製をお歳暮にもらって驚きましたが、信じられないほどおいしいものでした。

お歯黒
cosmetic tooth blackening 化粧目的での歯の黒塗り

Ohaguro is the ancient custom of blackening one's teeth that was popular during the Heian Period (794–1185) and was considered both fashionable and hygienic.

お歯黒とは、平安時代（794–1185年）に流行した、歯を黒くする古代の習慣のことで、おしゃれで衛生的だと考えられていた。

Hundreds of years ago, people dyed their teeth black as part of a **cosmetic tooth blackening** practice, so I wonder if it would be appropriate to call today's prevalent teeth-whitening "ohajiro."

何百年も前、人々はお歯黒の習慣の一環として歯を黒く塗っていました。だから、今日はやりの歯のホワイトニングのことは、「お歯白」と呼んではどうかと思うのです。

お七夜
baby naming ceremony 赤ん坊の名付け儀式

Oshichiya is the tradition of announcing a baby's name to close relatives, usually on the seventh night after the baby's birth.

お七夜とは、赤ん坊が生まれて7日目の夜に、近親者にその子の名前を発表する風習のこと。

Because my father had practiced calligraphy for many years, I was thrilled when he offered to write my new daughter's name for her **baby naming ceremony.**

父は長年書道をたしなんでいて、私の娘のお七夜のために名前を書いてやろうと言ってくれたので、私は感激しました。

お食い初め
baby food-tasting ceremony 赤ん坊の試食儀式

Okuizome is a tradition whereby around the 100th day after a baby is born, the baby is mock-fed an extravagant meal to express the hope that the baby will never want for food.

お食い初めとは、赤ん坊が生まれて100日目頃に、食べ物に困らないようにとの願いを込めて、豪華な食事を模擬的に食べさせる風習のこと。

At the **baby food-tasting ceremony**, we laughed when our three-year-old admonished our baby with a "*Mottainai!*" for not actually eating the food.

お食い初めの席で、うちの3歳の子供が、料理を本当には食べなかった赤ん坊を「もったいない！」といさめたのには笑ってしまいました。

034

お土産
souvenirs for others 他人への土産物

Omiyage are souvenirs—often sweets or savory snacks—bought for one's friends, family, colleagues, or customers.

お土産とは、友人や家族、同僚、顧客などのために買う土産物——たいてい菓子やスナック類——のことである。

It always brightened Esther's day when her *eikaiwa* students offered her a taste of Japan through **souvenirs for others** purchased from the far corners of the country.

英会話教室の生徒たちが、国内のいろいろな場所からお土産を買ってきて、日本の味覚を提供してくれると、エスターはいつも明るい気分になりました。

お年玉
New Year's gelt 新年のお金

Otoshidama are cash gifts given to children by adult relatives on New Year's.

お年玉とは、正月に親戚の大人が子供に贈る現金のこと。

While my kids always looked forward to the cash, whenever they received **New Year's gelt** from their grandparents, I always took pleasure in the decorative envelopes that were picked out.

祖父母からお年玉をもらうたびに、うちの子供たちはその金額に期待を寄せる一方、私はいつも、使われた飾り封筒を見るのが楽しみでした。

かっぱ
mythical amphibious imp 架空の水陸両生小鬼

Kappa are mythical water spirits with greenish-yellow skin, webbed hands and feet, and a carapace on their backs.

かっぱは神話に出てくる水の精霊で、緑がかった黄色い肌と水かきのある手足を持ち、背中に甲羅を背負っている。

I've been told that if I ever come face to face with a **mythical amphibious imp**, it is important for me to bow.

万が一、かっぱと対面することがあれば、おじぎをすることが大切だと言われたことがあります。

じゃんけん
rock paper scissors 石・紙・はさみ

The rules of *janken* may be no different from the game of rock, paper, scissors, but the practice is a cultural keystone in Japan, as it is often used when making major decisions or settling a variety of disputes.

じゃんけんのルールは、石・紙・はさみのゲームと変わらないかもしれないが、この慣行は日本の文化の要の一つだ。というのも、重大な決断を下すときや、さまざまな争いを解決するときにしばしば使われるからである。

Because his younger sister always chose rock, the boy was assured victory whenever they settled a dispute via **rock paper scissors**.

妹が必ずグーを出すので、その少年はじゃんけんで彼女とのけんかに決着をつけるとき、いつも勝利を確信しました。

なまはげ
New Year's ogre 新年の鬼

Namahage are a type of red- or blue-skinned ogre that descend from the mountains on New Year's Eve in search of children who have misbehaved during the year.

なまはげは赤や青の肌を持つ鬼の一種で、大みそかになると、その年に悪さをした子供たちを探して山から下りてくる。

When the **New Year's ogre** entered Ami's house, her young son cried in terror, but she managed to placate the demon with some delicious *sake*.

なまはげがアミの家に入ってくると、彼女の幼い息子は恐怖のあまり泣き出してしまいましたが、彼女はおいしい日本酒でどうにかその鬼をなだめました。

ねぶた祭り
colorful float festival カラフルな山車祭り

Aomori Prefecture's **Nebuta Matsuri**, one of the three largest festivals in northern Japan, features massive colorful floats depicting images from *kabuki* stories and Japanese myth.

青森県のねぶた祭りは、東北3大祭りの一つに数えられ、歌舞伎や日本の神話のイメージを模した巨大で色とりどりの山車が目玉である。

I may not know much about the history behind the **colorful float festival** floats, but I never fail to be impressed by their grandeur.

ねぶた祭りの山車にまつわる歴史はよく知らないのですが、その迫力にはいつも感動させられます。

のし
origami gift ornament 折り紙の贈答品用飾り

Noshi is a type of ornamental *origami* attached to gifts.

のしは、贈答品に付ける装飾用の折り紙の一種である。

When I gave my host family a souvenir from Japan, they admired the **origami gift ornament** so much that they put it in a frame and hung it on their wall.

私がホストファミリーに日本からのお土産を渡したら、彼らはのしをとても気に入り、額に入れて壁に飾ったのです。

ひな人形
Girls' Festival doll 桃の節句人形

Hinaningyō are dolls displayed for Girls' Day, on which families pray for their young daughters' health and happiness.

ひな人形とは、幼い娘の健康と幸せを家族で願うひな祭りの日に飾られる人形のこと。

Chisato's grandparents decided not to take out the **Girls' Festival dolls** on Girls' Day anymore because they take so long to arrange.

チサトの祖父母は、ひな祭りにひな人形を出さないことに決めました。並べるのに時間がかかりすぎるからです。

ホワイトデー
Valentine's Day reciprocity バレンタインデーの返礼

Howaitodē is the day on which men who received Valentine's Day gifts are obligated to reciprocate.

ホワイトデーは、バレンタインデーの贈り物をもらった男性が義務的に返礼する日である。

Saitō-san always arranged to be away from work during Valentine's Day in an effort to avoid having to reciprocate on the day of **Valentine's Day reciprocity**.

サイトウさんは、バレンタインデーのお返しをしなくてすむように、いつもバレンタインデーには職場から外出していました。

ラジオ体操
radio calisthenics exercises ラジオ柔軟体操

Rajiotaisō is a series of warm-up calisthenics performed to and guided by a particular melody.

ラジオ体操とは、特定のメロディーに合わせ、導かれながら行う一連の準備体操のこと。

Although I graduated from school decades ago, whenever I hear the **radio calisthenics exercises** music, I can't help but start swinging my arms.

もう何十年も前に学校を卒業しているにもかかわらず、ラジオ体操の音楽が聞こえると、つい腕を振ってしまいます。

茅の輪くぐり
grass hoop purification 草の輪によるおはらい

Chinowa kuguri is a purification ritual that takes place at Shintō shrines whereby people walk through a large ring made of woven grass.

茅の輪くぐりとは、神社で行われるおはらいの儀式の一つで、草で編んだ大きな輪を歩いてくぐる。

As a child, my siblings and I liked to do **grass hoop purification**, imagining ourselves going through a portal to another dimension.

子供の頃、私ときょうだいたちは茅の輪くぐりが好きで、異次元への扉をくぐる自分たちを想像していました。

干支
twelve-year Chinese zodiac 12年の中国式黄道十二宮

Eto are the zodiacal animals representing different years in a 12-year cycle.

干支とは、12年周期で異なる年を表す獣帯のこと。

My cousin and I may have the same **twelve-year Chinese zodiac** sign, but our personalities could not be more different.

いとこと私は干支が同じかもしれないけれど、性格はこれ以上ないほど違います。

鬼ごっこ
game of tag 鬼ごっこ遊び

With a history spanning more than 1,000 years, *onigokko* and its many variations are similar to the game of tag.

1,000年以上の歴史を持つ鬼ごっことその多くのバリエーションは、(西洋の) tag of war に似ている。

Whenever we go to the park, the first thing my kids always want to do is play **game of tag**.

一緒に公園に行くと、うちの子供たちはいつも最初に鬼ごっこをしたがります。

祇園祭
epidemic-repelling month-long festival
疫病を追い払う1カ月間の祭り

Originating as a purification ritual during an epidemic in 869 AD, *Gion Matsuri* is now one of the largest and most famous festivals in Japan.

西暦869年に流行した疫病の厄払いの儀式として始まった祇園祭は、現在では日本で最大かつ最も有名な祭りの一つである。

It has been suggested that the **epidemic-repelling month-long festival** hints that one of the ancient lost tribes of Israel found its way to Japan.

祇園祭は、古代イスラエルの失われた部族の一つが日本にたどり着いたことを示唆していると言われてきました。

きゅう
burning mugwort treatment 燃えるヨモギの治療

Kyū is a traditional Chinese medicine therapy that involves burning dried mugwort on particular points on the body.

きゅうは伝統的な中国医学の療法で、乾燥させたヨモギを体の特定のツボに据える。

Cody had his reservations when it came to **burning mugwort treatment**, but after a few applications, his arthritis became a thing of the past.

コーディーは、きゅうについては疑いを抱いていたのですが、数回据えてもらった後、関節炎が過去のものとなりました。

指圧
finger pressure massage 指の圧力マッサージ

Shiatsu, literally translated as "finger pressure," is a type of massage that primarily makes use of fingers and palms to apply pressure to various parts of the body.

指圧は、直訳すると「指の圧力」で、主に指や手のひらを使って体のいろいろな部位に圧力を加えるマッサージの一種である。

Nico was worried that **finger pressure massage** would translate to pain around his pressure points, but to his surprise, all his stress simply melted away.

ニコは、指圧がツボ周辺の痛みにつながるのではないかと心配していましたが、驚いたことに、ストレスがすっかり消えてなくなったのです。

元号
Japanese era name 日本の時代名

Gengō are the names of the eras in Japan and, since 1868, have reflected the length of each emperor's reign.

元号は、日本の時代の名称で、1868年以降、各天皇の在位期間を反映している。

The duration of modern **Japanese era names** suggests a period of relative social stability.

現代の元号の継続期間の長さは、社会が比較的安定している時期であることを示しています。

五月人形
Boys' Festival doll 端午の節句人形

Gogatsuningyō are the warrior figurines and other Japanese military regalia displayed before and during Boys' Festival on May 5 in honor of a household's sons.

五月人形は、5月5日の端午の節句の前と当日に飾られる武者人形やその他の日本の武具である。

The first time I saw the **Boys' Festival dolls** at my in-laws' house, I couldn't help but utter, "Awwwwwwwesommmmmmme!"

義理の両親の家で初めて五月人形を見たとき、私は思わず「すっごーい！」と叫んでしまいました。

こいのぼり
colorful carp-shaped windsock
カラフルなコイの形の吹き流し

Koinobori are carp-shaped windsocks flown to celebrate the national holiday known as Children's Day.

こいのぼりはコイの形の吹き流しで、祝日である「こどもの日」を祝うために掲げられる。

When Michael hung **colorful carp-shaped windsocks** outside his house in rural Texas, all the neighbors wondered what it meant.

マイケルがテキサス郊外の自宅の外にこいのぼりを掲げると、近所の人たちは皆、それは何を意味するのだろうかと不思議に思いました。

七五三
rite-of-passage children's festival 通過儀礼的子供の祭り

Shichigosan, literally translated as "seven five three," is a traditional rite of passage held on November 15 to celebrate the health of three- and seven-year-old girls and five-year-old boys.

七五三は、直訳すると「7・5・3」で、3歳と7歳の女の子と5歳の男の子の健康を祝うために11月15日に行われる、伝統的な通過儀礼である。

There are few things more adorable in this world than three-year-old girls dressed up in kimono for the **rite-of-passage children's festival**.

七五三の着物姿の3歳の女の子ほど、この世で愛らしいものはありません。

七十二候
pentad calendar divisions 5つの歴の区分

Shichijūnikō, literally translated as "72 climates," is an agricultural calendar divided into 72 pentads to describe seasonal shifts, both small and subtle.

七十二候は、直訳すれば「72の気候」で、季節の移り変わりを72の五節に分けた農事暦である。

There is something mystical and even magical about the **pentad calendar divisions**, its distinct poetry reverberating with the spirit of ancient Japan.

七十二候は、神秘的で呪術的でさえあり、その独特の優美さは日本古来の精神と響き合っています。

七夕祭り
star wish festival 星に願を掛ける祭り

Tanabata matsuri is an event that occurs in most places on July 7, celebrating the heavenly meeting of the star-crossed lovers Orihime and Hikoboshi.

七夕祭りは、大半の地域で7月7日に行われる行事で、星を隔てた恋人たち、織姫と彦星の天国での出会いを祝うものである。

As a child, I took the opportunity of the **star wish festival** to wish for frivolous things like superpowers or infinite tacos, but as an adult, my wishes were focused on the health and happiness of my children.

子供の頃、七夕祭りは、超能力や無限に食べられるタコスなどという軽薄なものを手に入れることを願う機会でしたが、大人になると、私の願い事は自分の子供たちの健康と幸せに集約されました。

除夜の鐘
end-of-year bell-ringing ceremony 年末の鐘鳴らし儀式

Joyanokane is the custom of ringing a temple bell at the turn of the year 108 times, symbolizing the 108 earthly temptations described by Buddhism.

除夜の鐘とは、年の変わり目に寺の鐘を108回突く風習のことで、仏教が説く108の煩悩を象徴している。

Aside from the Hakone Ekiden, the only New Year's television programming I truly look forward to is the **end-of-year bell-ringing ceremonies**.

箱根駅伝を除けば、私が心から楽しみにしている正月のテレビ放送は除夜の鐘の中継だけです。

新年会
New Year's party 新年の宴会

Shinnenkai, the companion to *bōnenkai*, are social gatherings—usually involving alcohol—held among friends or coworkers to celebrate the start of a new year.

新年会は忘年会と対をなすもので、友人や同僚と──通常は酒をくみ交わしながら──新年の始まりを祝う社交の場である。

By the end of the **New Year's party**, I was skipping around the room with a pair of underwear—hopefully my own—on my head.

新年会が終わるころには、私は下着──自分のものであってほしい──を頭にかぶって部屋の中をスキップして回ってしまいました。

神楽
Shintō ceremonial dance　神道の儀礼的舞踊

039

Kagura, literally translated as "god entertainment," is a ritualistic dance accompanied by music and dedicated to Shintō gods.

神楽は、直訳すれば「神の娯楽」で、神道の神々に捧げられる、音楽を伴った儀式的な舞踊である。

It is said that a female shaman that performs the **Shintō ceremonial dance** becomes herself a god during the performance.

神楽を舞う巫女は、舞いの最中に自分が神になると言われています。

水引
decorative knot-tying art　飾り結び術

Mizuhiki are ornamental rice paper cords that are tied around gifts and envelopes.

水引とは、贈答品や封筒に巻き付ける、わら紙で作った装飾用のひものこと。

Not knowing the significance of the different **decorative knot-tying art**, Jon almost purchased a funerary envelope for his friend's wedding.

さまざまな水引があり、それぞれ意味が異なることを知らなかったジョンは、友人の結婚式のために香典袋を購入しそうになりました。

接待
business partner entertainment 仕事相手のもてなし

🔵 ***Settai*** is the practice of wining and dining business associates for the purpose of forging and strengthening business relationships.

接待とは、ビジネス上の関係を築き強化する目的で、仕事の関係者を飲食でもてなす習慣のこと。

💬 At first, regular **business partner entertainment** on the company dime seemed like a dream come true, but after a few months of nearly daily entertainment, Mikey seriously worried about the state of his liver.

最初は会社のお金で定期的に人を接待することが夢のように思えたのに、数カ月間ほぼ毎日接待を続けたマイキーは、自分の肝臓の状態が本気で心配になりました。

節分
bean-throwing sushi-eating festival
豆を投げ、すしを食べる祭り

🔵 ***Setsubun***, literally translated as "seasonal division," is a festival for welcoming good fortune and driving evil spirits away, and it takes place the day before *Risshun*, the first day of spring according to the Japanese lunar calendar.

節分は、直訳すると「季節の分かれ目」で、福を迎え、邪気をはらう祭りを指す。日本の旧暦における立春の前日に行われる。

💬 Kyle's favorite part of **bean-throwing sushi-eating festival** is wolfing down a massive roll of *makizushi*.

カイルが節分で一番気に入っている点は、大きな巻きずしを頬張ることです。

040

選び取り
future selection ritual　未来の選別儀式

Erabitori is a ritual whereby items representing potential life callings are arrayed in front of a baby, and the baby is encouraged to choose one to give insight into her or his future path.

選び取りとは、目の前に並べられた潜在的な職業を表す品々の中から、赤ん坊に自分の将来の道筋を見通すものを選ばせる儀式のこと。

Everyone laughed during the **future selection ritual** ceremony when the baby grabbed the spoon and immediately put it in his mouth.

選び取りの場で、赤ちゃんがスプーンをつかむと、すぐに口に入れたので、皆が笑いました。

滝行
ascetic waterfall meditation　修行のための滝の瞑想

Takigyō is a form of ascetic meditation that involves cleansing one's mind, body, and soul under the rush of a waterfall.

滝行とは、流れ落ちる滝の水の下で心身や魂を清める、修行のための瞑想のこと。

Despite—or perhaps due to—the near-freezing temperatures and the deafening roar of the water, Noah felt free and detached from material woes as he was pummeled by the waterfall during his **ascetic waterfall meditation** experience.

氷点下に近い気温と耳をつんざく水のごう音にもかかわらず――あるいはおそらくそのせいで――ノアは滝行の体験で水に打たれながら、物質的な苦悩から解き放たれ、自由を感じました。

photo: Takashi Ueki

タヌキ
legendary big-balled mischief-maker
伝説的な睾丸の大きないたずら者

🔵 The *tanuki* is a species of canid endemic to Japan with a reputation for mischief.

タヌキは日本固有のイヌ科の動物で、いたずら好きで知られている。

💬 Many a visitor to Japan has delighted in the image of a **legendary big-balled mischief-maker** with its comically large testicles, practically the size of beanbag chairs.

日本を訪れた多くの人が大喜びするのが、ほとんどビーンバッグチェア並みの大きさの、こっけいなほど大きな睾丸を持つタヌキの姿です。

てんぐ
mischievous long-nosed creature
いたずら好きの鼻の長い生き物

🔵 *Tengu* are supernatural beings characterized by arrogance and mischief, often depicted with red faces and unnaturally long noses.

てんぐは傲慢でいたずら好きな超自然的な生き物で、たいてい赤い顔と不自然に長い鼻を持った姿で描かれる。

💬 People's perceptions of the **mischievous long-nosed creature** have changed over time: what were once supernatural mischief-makers became vigilant protectors of the land.

人々が抱くてんぐのイメージは、時代とともに変わってきました。かつては超自然的でいたずら好きだったものが、用心深い土地の守り神になりました。

桃太郎
Peach Boy Hero 英雄モモ少年

Momotarō is a well-known folklore hero who was born from a giant peach and went on a number of adventures.

桃太郎は有名な民間伝承の英雄で、巨大なモモから生まれた後、数々の冒険を繰り広げた。

I wonder if **Peach Boy Hero** and James from *James and the Giant Peach* ever met.

桃太郎と『ジャイアント・ピーチ』のジェームズは会ったことがあるのでしょうか。

妖怪
supernatural mythical being 超自然的な架空の生き物

Yōkai are supernatural beings of Japanese folklore.

妖怪は、日本の民間伝承に出てくる超自然的な生き物である。

Supernatural mythical beings may be scary and unsettling to some, but I wished for an *akaname* to visit at night to spare me the trouble of cleaning my bath.

妖怪は恐ろしく、不安をあおるかもしれませんが、私は風呂掃除の手間を省いてくれるアカナメが夜、うちの風呂場を訪れてくれることを願いました。

年賀状
New Year's card 新年のはがき

Nengajō are New Year's postcards sent to friends, family, business partners, and clients to convey season's greetings and well wishes.

年賀状とは新年のはがきのことで、友人、家族、取引先、顧客などに季節のあいさつや幸福への祈りを伝えるために送られる。

Some people relish the convenience of a digital **New Year's card**, but I appreciate the thoughtfulness that goes into a handwritten card.

デジタル年賀状の利便性を好む人もいますが、私は手書きの年賀状に込められた心遣いをありがたく感じます。

盆栽
potted miniature tree 鉢植えの小型樹木

Bonsai, which literally translates to "tray-planted," is the horticultural practice of cutting a tree or shrub in such a way as to give the impression of it being a full-sized, mature tree despite its diminutive size.

盆栽は、直訳すると「盆で栽培される」で、木や低木を、小さなサイズにもかかわらず、あたかも一回り大きく成長した樹木であるかのように剪定する園芸手法である。

After Irving passed on, his favorite grandson inherited his collection of **potted miniature trees**, maintaining them meticulously just as Irving had.

アービングが亡くなった後、最愛の孫が彼の
盆栽コレクションを受け継ぎ、アービングと
同じように丹念に手入れをしました。

盆踊り
spirit welcome dance 霊を歓迎する踊り

042

Bon-odori refers to a range of dances performed during *obon*, the annual summer event during which people honor their ancestors and welcome their spirits back home.

盆踊りとは、お盆の時期に踊られるいろいろな舞踏のことで、先祖を敬い、霊を故郷に迎える夏の恒例行事である。

The way the **spirit welcome dance** hums with energy and rhythm, I could almost believe that the spirits of our ancestors really feel it.

盆踊りがエネルギーとリズムに満ちている様子は、先祖の霊が本当にそれを感じられるのではないかと思えるほどです。

鈴
hollow Shintō bell 中空の神道のベル

A *suzu* is a round, hollow bell that contains pellets that produce a sound when shaken, similar to a sleigh bell.

鈴とは、丸い中空のベルのことで、振ると音が鳴るペレットが入っており、そりのベルに似ている。

At first, I thought I heard the jingling of Santa's sleigh, but then I realized it was just the **hollow Shintō bell** from a nearby shrine.

最初、サンタクロースのそりのジャラジャラという音が聞こえたような気がしたのですが、すぐに近くの神社の鈴の音だと気づきました。

Chapter
3

Clothing/Fashion/Culture
服装・流行・文化

キモかわいい

creepy and cute
ゾッとしてかわいい

文で説明してみよう！

Kimokawaii describes something that is simultaneously gross and cute, as enticing as it is disturbing.

キモカワイイとは、グロテスクなさまとかわいさを同時に表現したもので、嫌な感じあると同時に魅力的なことである。

3語フレーズを会話で使おう！

Maybe it's a cultural thing, but to Alex, characters considered **creepy and cute** in Japan are just plain gross.

たぶん文化の違いなのでしょうが、アレックスにとって、日本でキモかわいいとされるキャラクターはただ気持ち悪いだけです。

Andrew's Point

The most difficult part of this term was neither of the adjectives. "Cute" was obvious, and I felt "creepy" was slightly more apt than "gross" (although "gross" could certainly work to some extent). The problem was the conjunction. I started with "but" until I realized that it's not a juxtaposition of two opposing qualities; it's two qualities that fuse in an unexpected harmony. And I say unexpected because, at first, I had no love for *kakure-momojiri* or any of his friends. But they grew on me. I would never call one of those characters just "cute" or just "creepy." It's an absurd but alluring *kimokawaii* mix.

この言葉で一番難しかったのは、2つの形容詞の部分ではありませんでした。**cute** が使えるのは明らかで、**creepy** のほうが **gross** よりも若干適切だと感じました（**gross** でもある程度はいけるでしょうが）。問題は接続詞だったのです。最初は **but** としたのですが、やがてこれが相反する2つの性質の並置ではなく、2つの性質が予想外に調和し融合しているのだと気づきました。予想外に、と言ったのは、当初私はカクレモモジリにもその友人たちにも、何の愛着も湧かなかったからです。しかし、やがて私の中で彼らの存在が大きくなりました。ああいうキャラクターを単に **cute** あるいは単に **creepy** とは決して呼べません。ばかげているけれど魅力的なキモかわいい融合体なのです。

ギャル

044

gaudy female fashion

けばけばしい女性ファッション

 文で説明してみよう！

Gyaru is a fashion subculture that emerged in the late 1990s and is characterized by bleached hair, tanned skin, short skirts, and heavy makeup.

ギャルとは、1990年代後半に現れたファッションサブカルチャーのことで、脱色した髪、日焼けした肌、短いスカート、濃い化粧が特徴である。

 3語フレーズを会話で使おう！

Her university life nearing completion, Aya had to dye her hair black and bid farewell to her **gaudy female fashion** before she started to search for a job.

大学生活が終わりに近づき、アヤは髪を黒く染め、ギャルのイメージを捨てて就職活動を始めました。

Andrew's Point

Gyaru was more than just a particular fashion. It was an attitude, an assertion of individuality and self-expression. It was a rebellion against traditional beauty standards and a celebration of youthful exuberance. And while it was certainly gaudy by some measures, that made it no less iconic or impactful. These days, when I see pictures of *gyaru* from the 1990s, they evoke the same nostalgia as leafing through my old junior high school and high school yearbooks (I graduated from high school in 1997). I didn't live in Japan then, but I hear and feel the echoes of the past just the same.

ギャルとは単なる一ファッションを超えたものでした。それは1つの主張であり、個性や自己表現を示すことでした。伝統的な美の基準への反抗であり、若さあふれる高揚の賛美でした。そして、確かにある基準に照らせば派手ではあったものの、だからといって偶像的あるいは影響力に満ちたものではありませんでした。今になって、1990年代のギャルの写真を見ると、自分の中学や高校の卒業アルバム（私は1997年に高校を卒業しました）を見返すのと同じようなノスタルジーを呼び起こされます。当時は日本に住んでいませんでしたが、同じように過去の残響が聞こえたり感じられたりするのです。

コスプレ

fantasy dress-up roleplaying

ファンタジーの着飾った役割演技

文で説明してみよう！

Kosupure, a portmanteau of "costume" and "play," is an activity in which participants dress up and act as characters from *anime*, *manga*, video games, and other media.

コスプレとは、costume と play の合成語で、アニメや漫画、ビデオゲームなどのキャラクターに扮装してその役を演じる行為のことである。

3語フレーズを会話で使おう！

Once a geeky niche, **fantasy dress-up roleplaying** has come to enjoy worldwide attention.

かつてはマニアックでニッチだったコスプレは、今や世界的な注目を集めるようになっています。

Andrew's Point

I once paid a prop designer a significant amount of money to make a Master Roshi (from *Dragon Ball*) costume for me. It was a work of art. The staff unscrewed in the middle so I could pack it into luggage, and when I put it back together, it was seamless. The purple shell looked like it came straight out of the *Dragon Ball anime*. I was going to role-play my heart out! I was going to win costume contests! I was going to make exciting new friends! But… it smelled. Whatever materials the prop designer used gave off an unpleasant chemical odor so severe that I thought I might be damaging my lungs. I aired it out for over a year to no avail. Ultimately, I had to throw it away.

以前、小道具デザイナーにかなりの金額を払って、(『ドラゴンボール』の) 亀仙人のコスチュームを作ってもらったことがあります。それは芸術品でした。梱包できるようにスタッフが中間部でネジを外してくれたのですが、元に戻してみると継ぎ目が見えないほどでした。紫色の甲羅はドラゴンボールのアニメからそのまま出てきたようでした。私は役になり切るつもりでした！ コスチュームコンテストで優勝しようと思っていたのです！ ワクワクするような新しい友だちを作るつもりでした！ でも……臭かったのです。その小道具デザイナーが使った素材が何であれ、不快な化学臭を放つので、肺を傷めてしまうのではないかと思うほどでした。1年以上干しても効果がありませんでした。結局、捨てるしかなくなってしまったのです。

パパ活

046

sugar daddy hunting

男性パトロン狩り

 文で説明してみよう！

Papakatsu is the act of girls finding sugar daddies to shower them with gifts, money, and expensive meals just for the pleasure of their company.

パパ活とは、女の子たちがパトロンを見つける行為のことで、パトロンには、自分と一緒に過ごす楽しみだけのためにプレゼントやお金、高価な食事などを惜しげもなく与えてもらう。

 3語フレーズを会話で使おう！

At the restaurant, there was a couple that had such a stark difference in age that I couldn't help but wonder if the woman was engaging in **sugar daddy hunting**.

そのレストランには、あまりにも年齢差の大きいカップルがいて、女性のほうがパパ活をしているのではないかと疑わずにはいられませんでした。

Andrew's Point

A "sugar daddy" refers to an older man who offers financial and/or material support—the "sugar"—to a younger person, often referred to as a "sugar baby," in exchange for companionship, intimacy, or other forms of attention. It slightly differs from *papakatsu* in that the relationship is more transactional in nature and there is a clear understanding of mutual benefits. It's interesting to me that despite the existence of the terms and even apps and websites meant to facilitate the finding of "sugar daddies" in the West, there is no recognized English term for looking for a sugar daddy (or sugar mama, in some cases).

sugar daddyとは、しばしばsugar babyと呼ばれる年下の女性に対して、交際や親密な関係、その他の行為と引き換えに、金銭的・物質的な援助──「砂糖」のように甘いもの──を提供する年長の男性のことを指します。関係がよりビジネスライクで、相互の利益について当事者間で明確な理解があるという点で、パパ活とは少し異なります。欧米にはsugar daddyを見つけやすくするための言葉や、さらにはアプリ、ウェブサイトまで存在するにもかかわらず、sugar daddy（場合によってはsugar mama）を探す活動を表す一般的な英語の表現がないのは面白いと思います。

ふんどし

traditional men's thong

伝統的な男性用ひも状下着

文で説明してみよう！

A **fundoshi** is a traditional cotton loincloth that was considered mainstream underwear for men in Japan until World War II.

ふんどしは伝統的な木綿の腰巻き布で、第二次世界大戦まで日本では男性の下着の主流とされていた。

３語フレーズを会話で使おう！

While Clyde wasn't the least bit embarrassed bathing naked at an *onsen*, when he was told he'd have to wear a **traditional men's thong** at the upcoming festival, his face turned beet red.

クライドは裸で温泉に入るのは少しも恥ずかしくありませんでしたが、今度のお祭りではふんどしを締めなければならないと言われ、顔を真っ赤にしました。

Andrew's Point

During my first year in Japan, I was fortunate to see and participate in a number of exciting local festivals. I distinctly remember going to one festival where the men were all wearing traditional thong underwear. "I want to wear *fundoshi* at a festival!" I immediately declared, and my friend burst out laughing. "Hahaha! No one wants to see your hairy gorilla butt!" she said. Maybe she was right, and, in fact, I don't have the confidence to go to a beach and wear a men's thong *bikini*. But at a festival, where traditional thong underwear is expected, I think I'd be fine with it. It's like the first time I went to an *onsen*. In America, the thought of getting naked with friends and relaxing in a hot spring is considered ludicrous. But in Japan? It's no big deal. Culture is funny like that.

日本に暮らし始めた最初の1年間、私は幸運にも地元のエキサイティングな祭りをいくつも見たり、それらに参加したりすることができました。ある祭りに行ったとき、男性陣が皆、伝統的なひも状の下着を身に着けていたのを鮮明に覚えています。「祭りでふんどしを履きたい！」と私が即座に宣言すると、友人は大笑いしました。「ハハハ！ 誰もあなたの毛深いゴリラみたいなお尻なんて見たくないわよ！」と言うのです。たぶん彼女の言うとおりで、実際、ビーチに行って男性用のTバックビキニを着る自信はありません。でも、伝統的なひも状の下着を身に着けることになっている祭りでは、平気だと思います。初めて温泉に行ったときのような感じでしょう。アメリカでは、友達と裸になって温泉でくつろぐなど、おかしなことだと思われています。でも日本では？ どうということはありません。文化とは、このように面白いものなのです。

リクルートスーツ

048

job interview suit

就職面接用スーツ

 文で説明してみよう！

Rikurūto sūtsu, derived from the English words "recruit" and "suit," are conservative black suits typically worn by job-seekers for their job interviews.

リクルートスーツとは、英語のrecruitとsuitに由来するもので、就職活動をする人が面接の際に着用する保守的な黒いスーツのことである。

 ３語フレーズを会話で使おう！

I thought I'd make an impression by wearing some colorful socks along with my **job interview suit**, but the interviewers were so put off that I didn't get hired anywhere I applied.

リクルートスーツにカラフルな靴下を履いて印象を良くしようと思ったのですが、面接官たちは引いてしまい、応募したところはどこも私を採用してくれませんでした。

Andrew's Point

I once worked at an especially conservative Japanese company that enforced a strict dress code. I violated that dress code every single day of my employment with brightly colored socks as an act of defiance against what I saw as a meaningless attempt to suppress individuality. I saw no point in conforming being that I was already a spectacle as the only foreign employee among a staff of hundreds. I was different and it shouldn't have mattered. But I understand that in some cases, adhering to the norm is safe. It can be essential for fostering a unified corporate identity. A job interview suit broadcasts to potential employers, "I am trustworthy, stable, and reliable." I suppose I wasn't. I quit that job within the year.

私は以前、とりわけ保守的な日本企業で働いていました。私は、個性を抑えようとする無意味な試みへの反抗として、明るい色の靴下をはいて、毎日ドレスコードを破っていました。何百人もいるスタッフの中で唯一の外国人従業員として、すでに見世物になっていた私が、周囲に合わせる意味はないと思いました。私は人と違うのだから、そんなことはどうでもいいはずだと。でも、規範を守ることが安全な場合もあることは理解しています。統一された企業人としてのアイデンティティーを育むためには、それが不可欠なこともあります。リクルートスーツは、将来の雇用主に「私は信用できます、安定しています、頼りになります」とアピールするものです。どうやら私は違ったようです。私はその仕事を1年以内に辞めました。

旧車会

old-school motorcycle enthusiasts

旧来のオートバイ熱狂者たち

文で説明してみよう！

Kyūshakai are groups of motorcycle aficionados that enjoy riding together on customized motorcycles.

旧車会とはオートバイ愛好家のグループのことで、カスタマイズしたオートバイに乗り集団で走ることを楽しむ。

3語フレーズを会話で使おう！

Whatever you may think of the motorcycles of **old-school motorcycle enthusiasts**, their fashion is often a wonder to behold.

旧車会のオートバイについてどう思うかはともかく、彼らのファッションにはしばしば目を見張るものがあります。

Andrew's Point

I wanted to take special care here to differentiate *kyūshakai* from *bōsōzoku*. Certainly, there may be some overlap—both can be frighteningly noisy and quite intimidating—but I wanted to stress that *kyūshakai* is focused on the love of old-school motorcycles rather than violence. I also like that while "old-school" describes the vehicles themselves, members of *kyūshakai* tend to be older than *bōsōzoku*, lending "old-school" a double meaning. (Were it not for the double meaning, I might have gone with "retro" instead.) I have a lot of respect for *kyūshakai* and I even enjoy their catchy idling rhythms. But not so much at 3 a.m.

私はここで、旧車会と暴走族を区別するために特別な注意を払いたかったのです。確かに、どちらも恐ろしくうるさかったり、威圧的だったりするので、重なる部分があるかもしれませんが、旧車会は暴力よりも、旧式のオートバイへの愛に重点を置いていることを強調したいと思いました。また、**old-school**が車自体を形容する一方で、旧車会のメンバーがおおむね暴走族よりも年長であることも表し、結果的に**old-school**が二重の意味を持つ点に入っています(このダブルミーニングがなければ、代わりに**retro**という語を使ったかもしれません)。私は旧車会を尊敬しているし、彼らのキャッチーな空吹かしのリズムを楽しんでさえいます。でも、午前3時というのはちょっと。

女子会

all-female organized outing

女性だけの準備された外出

 文で説明してみよう！

A *joshikai* is a gathering just for women, whether it be a girls' night out or a casual chat over tea.

女子会とは、女性だけの集まりのことで、女子の夜会であっても、お茶を飲みながらの気軽なおしゃべり会であってもいい。

 ３語フレーズを会話で使おう！

Chihiro used to love letting off some steam with her high school friends at their regular **all-female organized outings**, but ever since she had kids, she was too exhausted to go out.

チヒロは以前、高校時代の友人たちとの定例の女子会で憂さ晴らしをするのが好きでした。でも、子供ができてからは、外出するのが億劫になってしまいました。

Andrew's Point

Obviously, not being a female, I've never been to a *joshikai*, so I can only use my imagination and reference guides to understand precisely what goes on. But I do know that it's not limited to later hours, so the expression "girls' night out" does not apply. This may be one of the only terms wherein a two-word phrase might've applied: "girls-only gathering." But I thought I could refine it with three. "All-female" removes any implied age restrictions, "organized" differentiates it from an impromptu event, and "outing" means that it's probably not just at someone's home. Or maybe it can be? As I said, I've never been a female nor been to a *joshikai* myself.

もちろん、私は女性ではないので、女子会に行ったことはありません。だから、想像力や参考文献を使わない限りは正確にはどんなことが行われているのか理解できません。しかし、遅い時間帯に限定されるものではないことは分かっているので、**girls' night out** のような表現は当てはまりません。これはもしかすると、2語のフレーズにすべき限られた言葉の一つかもしれません。つまり **girls-only gathering** です。しかし、私はこれを3語に整理できると考えました。**all-female** は暗黙の年齢制限を取り除き、**organized** は即席のイベントとは違うことを表現し、**outing** は会場が誰かの家だけではないことを伝えます。あるいは、そういったこともあり得るのでしょうか？ 先述のとおり、私自身、女性になったこともなければ、女子会に行ったこともありませんから何とも。

親父ギャグ

051

groan-inducing dad joke

不満の声を呼ぶお父さんの冗談

 文で説明してみよう！

Oyaji gyagu, literally translated as "dad jokes," are a type of Japanese pun.

親父ギャグとは、直訳すれば「父親の冗談」で、日本のダジャレの一種である。

 3 語フレーズを会話で使おう！

Is a punster's delight a product of the laughter or the suffering induced by a good old **groan-inducing dad joke**?

ダジャレ好きの喜びとは、笑いを生み出すものにあるのでしょうか、それとも昔ながらの親父ギャグがもたらす苦しみにあるのでしょうか。

Andrew's Point

As soon as I became a father and my kids were old enough to talk, it was as if it were predestined. "Daaaaad, I'm hungry." "Hi, Hungry! I'm Dad." (All English-speaking pun aficionados know this one.) It might be easy to dismiss *oyaji gyagu* as a cheap form of sadism, but *oyaji gyagu* have the power to turn the mundane into the memorable. It's a timeless tradition that helps fathers connect with their children with a shared chuckle or groan. Come to think of it, my mother, too, has fired off a few clever groaners from time to time. I suppose the fact that any mom or dad can make a good pun should be apPARENT. (Haha!)

私が父親になり、子供たちがおしゃべりのできる年齢になったとたん、それはまるで運命づけられているかのようでした。「パパー、僕はおなか空いた」「やあ、おなか空いたくん、僕はパパだよ」（英語圏のダジャレ愛好家なら誰でもこれを知っています）。親父ギャグを安っぽいサディズムの一種として否定するのは簡単かもしれませんが、親父ギャグには平凡なものを記憶に残るものに変える力があります。父親が子供たちと笑いやうなり声を分かち合うことで、子供たちと心を通わせることができるのです。そういえば、私の母もときどき、気の利いたダジャレを飛ばしていました。オヤ親、ダジャレが誰にでも言えるというのは事実らしいですね。（ハハハ！）

痛車

character-riddled automotive eyesore

キャラクターまみれの見苦しい自動車

文で説明してみよう！

Itasha, loosely translated as "cringe car," describes a vehicle decorated with images of characters and logos from *anime*, *manga*, or video games.

痛車とは、大まかに訳せば「恥ずかしい車」で、アニメや漫画、ゲームなどのキャラクターやロゴをあしらった車のこと。

3語フレーズを会話で使おう！

Frank enjoyed it whenever he saw a **character-riddled automotive eyesore** drive by, but he knew his parents would disown him if he ever got one of his own.

フランクは痛車が通り過ぎるのを見るたびに楽しんでいましたが、自分が痛車を手に入れたら両親に勘当されることは分かっていました。

Andrew's Point

Many people will agree that *itasha* are absolute eyesores. They simultaneously offend both art and traffic. The homage they pay to the *anime*, *manga*, and video game characters that adorn their bodies and interiors serves only to disgrace them. That's one opinion. But deep down, I think I secretly envy these *itasha* owners. What gives them the confidence to put their individuality on such a bold display? Or is it less confidence and more a total unconcern regarding the opinions of others? I can't imagine ever sharing my collection of Dragonball figures earned from convenience store lotteries with anyone but my children. But maybe I should shed such needless shame.

多くの人が、痛車が明らかに目障りであることに同意するでしょう。芸術と交通を同時に害するものです。車体や内装を飾る、アニメや漫画、ゲームのキャラクターへ向けたオマージュは、ただそれらをおとしめているだけです。これはあくまでも一つの見方です。しかし、心の底では、私はこうした痛車のオーナーたちを密かにうらやんでいるのです。何が彼らに、あそこまで大胆に個性を誇示できるだけの自信を与えるのか。あるいは、自信というより、他人の考えをまったく気にしないということなのか。コンビニのくじで手に入れたドラゴンボールのフィギュアのコレクションを、自分の子供以外に見せることなど、私には考えられません。でも、そんな無用な羞恥心は捨てるべきなのかもしれません。

053

げた
wooden clog flip-flops 木製靴型サンダル

Geta are traditional but informal wooden sandals with a flat wooden base, a fabric thong, and one to three teeth that keep the base up off the ground.

げたは伝統的でありながらカジュアルな木製のサンダルで、平らな木の土台、布製の鼻緒、土台を地面から浮かせるための1本から3本の歯が備わっている。

Shōko stopped complaining about her high heels once her grandmother suggested she try wearing one-toothed **wooden clog flip-flops** for the day.

ショウコは、祖母が丸一日1本歯のげたを履いてみるよう提案すると、ハイヒールに文句を言わなくなりました。

じんべい
Japanese-style home wear 和式ホームウエア

Jinbei are traditionally worn in the summer and feature a tube-sleeved kimono-style top and a pair of pants, all made of lightweight material.

じんべいは伝統的に夏に着用されるもので、筒袖の着物風の上半身とズボンが特徴である。どれも薄手の素材でできている。

Once Evan discovered **Japanese-style home wear**, he never went back to any other type of pajamas again.

一度じんべいを知ってしまったエバンは、もう他の種類のパジャマに戻れませんでした。

ダジャレ
low-grade groan-inducing pun
低レベルの不満の声を呼ぶシャレ

Dajare is a form of wordplay that makes use of the ambiguity between homophonic or near-homophonic Japanese words.

ダジャレとは、同音異義語やそれに近い日本語のあいまいさを利用した言葉遊びの一種である。

"Shōyū koto da!" Shintarō said, brandishing a bottle of soy sauce and eliciting a chorus of groans with his awful **low-grade groan-inducing pun**.

「しょうゆうことだ！」とシンタロウが、しょうゆの瓶を振り回しながらひどいダジャレを口に出すと、場が一斉にどよめきました。

デコトラ
kitschy tricked-out truck　どぎつく飾り立てられたトラック

Dekotora, a portmanteau of "decoration" and "truck," is a subculture wherein people deck out their trucks in a variety of often kitschy, eye-popping styles.

デコトラとは、decorationとtruckの合成語で、トラックをどぎつく、あっと驚くようなさまざまなスタイルで飾り付けるサブカルチャーのこと。

Izumi always loves seeing her young children's eyes light up when they see a flashy **kitschy tricked-out truck** drive by.

イズミはいつも、すれ違う派手なデコトラに、自分の幼い子供たちが目を輝かせる様子を見るのが大好きです。

photo: brunomiguel

054

パチンコ
plinko meets slots
プリンコとスロットマシーンの出合い

🗒 *Pachinko* is a recreational game that combines elements of slot machines and pinball along with visual and aural sensory overload.

パチンコは、スロットマシンやピンボールの要素と、視覚的・聴覚的な要素を過剰に組み合わせた娯楽ゲームである。

💬 The first time I went into a **plinko meets slots** parlor, I had to stop in the doorway as I walked face-first into a impenetrable wall of sound.

初めてパチンコ店に入ったとき、頑強な音の壁に顔面から突っ込み、入り口で立ち止まらざるを得ませんでした。

はっぴ
tube-sleeved festival coat 筒型袖の祭り用コート

🗒 *Happi* are loose-fitting, straight-sleeved coats often decorated with a distinctive crest and worn during festivals.

はっぴは、ゆったりとした真っすぐの袖を持つ上着で、独特の紋章があしらわれていることが多く、祭りの際に着用される。

💬 I could not have been more thrilled when within mere months of my arrival in Japan, I was participating in a local festival and wearing a **tube-sleeved festival coat**.

日本に来てわずか数カ月で、地元の祭りに参加し、はっぴを着たのですから、あれほどスリリングな経験は他にありません。

はんてん
Edo-period winter coat 江戸時代風冬季コート

Dating back to the 18th century, *hanten* are short winter unisex coats packed with a thick layer of wadded cotton for warmth.

はんてんは、18世紀に起源を持つ冬用の男女兼用の短いコートで、保温性を高めるために厚手の中綿が詰め込まれている。

When Tamar got lost in the *onsen* town, a helpful passerby found the name of her inn written on her **Edo-period winter coat**.

タマーが温泉街で道に迷ったとき、親切な通行人が彼女のはんてんに宿の名前が書いてあるのを見つけてくれました。

プリクラ
effects-laden photo booth エフェクト満載の写真ボックス

Purikura, a portmanteau of "purinto" (print) and "kurabu" (club), is a photo booth that offers a multitude of ways to customize and decorate photos and is a key staple of youth culture in Japan.

プリクラとは、「プリント（print）」と「クラブ（club）」の合成語で、写真をカスタマイズしたり装飾したりするさまざまな方法を提供するフォトブースであり、日本の若者文化の外せない定番設備である。

When the kids stepped out of the **effects-laden photo booth**, they cried with laughter when they saw how unrecognizably they had morphed their faces.

プリクラから出てきた子供たちは、自分の顔が見違えるほど変貌しているのを見て、大笑いしながら声を上げました。

055

やおい
male homoerotic media 男性同性愛メディア

Yaoi is a genre of fictional media depicting relationships, both romantic and sexual, between male characters.

やおいは、男性キャラクター同士の恋愛や性的な関係を描いたフィクションのメディアの一ジャンルである。

One reason fans of **male homoerotic media** enjoy the genre is that they are generally devoid of oversexualized female forms found in so much other media.

やおいのファンがこのジャンルを楽しむ理由の一つは、他の多くのメディアに見られるような、過剰に性的に表現された女性像がふつう避けられていることにあります。

ボディコン
sexually flattering clothing 性的に引き立たせる服装

Bodikon, a portmanteau of "body" and "conscious," is a style of tight, form-fitting clothing that was popular in Japan in the 1980s and 1990s.

ボディコンは、body と conscious の合成語で、1980年代から1990年代にかけて日本で流行したタイトで体にフィットした服のスタイルである。

Natsuki Okamoto, a race queen who helped popularize the **sexually flattering clothing** movement, largely disappeared from the public eye before staging a brief comeback in the early 2010s.

ボディコンムーブメントの普及に貢献したレースクイーンの岡本夏生は、2010年代初頭に一時的にカムバックを果たすまで、ほとんど表舞台から姿を消していました。

衣替え
seasonal wardrobe change 季節ごとの衣服の交換

Koromogae is the practice of swapping the previous season's wardrobe with one more suitable for the coming season.

衣替えとは、前シーズンの衣服を次のシーズンに適したものに入れ替えることである。

I've become so efficient with regard to how I store my clothes that I can do a complete **seasonal wardrobe change** in under ten minutes.

私はとても効率的に服を収納できる方法を身につけたので、10分以内に衣替えを完了できます。

羽織
medium-length kimono jacket
中ぐらいの丈の着物ジャケット

Resembling kimonos themselves, *haori* are formal hip- or thigh-length overcoats worn over a kimono.

それ自体が着物に似ている羽織は、着物の上に羽織る腰丈またはもも丈のフォーマルな上着である。

Medium-length kimono jackets could easily take off as a fashion trend in the U.S. if people weren't so overly concerned with cultural appropriation.

もしも人々が文化の盗用を過剰に心配していなければ、羽織はアメリカで簡単にファッショントレンドになり得ることでしょう。

056

援助交際
sugar daddy relationship 男性パトロン関係

Enjokōsai, which can be translated as "assisted relationship" or "compensated dating," is a type of transactional relationship whereby an older man gives money and luxury items to a young woman in exchange for sexual favors.

援助交際は「援助された関係」あるいは「報酬を伴うデート」と訳すことが可能で、年長の男性が若い女性に金銭やぜいたく品を与える代わりに性的な関係を結ぶという、取引関係の一種である。

As Akiko's friends gushed with envy over her new 300,000 yen handbag, she couldn't help but wonder what they would think of her if they discovered that it was the fruit of her secret **sugar daddy relationship**.

アキコは、友人たちが自分の30万円の新しいハンドバッグをうらやましそうに眺めているとき、もしそれが秘密の援助交際の成果だと分かったら、彼らは自分のことをどう思うだろうかと考えずにはいられませんでした。

かわいい
cute and adorable かわいくて愛らしい

Kawaii transcends the English idea of "cuteness," describing a culture where all things cute and adorable are celebrated.

かわいいは、英語のcutenessという概念を超越し、かわいいものや愛らしいもののすべてが賞賛される文化を表している。

Even though my oldest son is only four years old, he rejects being complimented as **cute and adorable**, instead preferring "cool."

私の長男はまだ4歳ですが、かわいいと褒められるのを嫌がり、「カッコイイ」と言われるほうを喜びます。

合コン
group blind date 集団ブラインドデート

Gōkon, a portmanteau of "gōdō" (mixed) and "konpa" (informal group meeting), is a group blind dating event designed to introduce an equal number of men and women over food and drinks.

合コンとは、「合同（mixed）」と「コンパ（カジュアルなグループ会合）」を合わせた造語で、食事や酒を楽しみながら同数の男女を引き合わせる集団お見合いイベントである。

Kaho may not have found a partner at the **group blind date**, but she felt fortunate to have made a good friend.

カホは、合コンでパートナーを見つけることはできなかったかもしれないけれど、良い友人ができたことを幸運に感じました。

雪駄
weaved bamboo sandals 編まれた竹のサンダル

Setta are durable sandals traditionally made with weaved bamboo and a leather sole.

雪駄は丈夫なサンダルで、伝統的に編んだ竹と革の底でできている。

Modern **weaved bamboo sandals** may have diverged from the materials of the past, but they are both chic and comfortable, the perfect footwear for a variety of occasions.

現代の雪駄はかつてとは異なる素材を用いているかもしれませんが、シックで履き心地が良く、さまざまな場面で申し分なく使える履物です。

057

扇子
traditional folding fan 伝統的な折りたたみ式うちわ

Invented more than 1,000 years ago and inspired by round fans from China, *sensu* are folding fans made of bamboo and Japanese paper.

1,000年以上前に発明され、中国の丸い扇にヒントを得た扇子は、竹と和紙で作られている。

I appreciate the air of refinement borne by the flutter of a **traditional folding fan**, but in the dead of summer, I opt for a high-powered air conditioner set to full blast.

扇子のはためきが生み出す上品な風は好きですが、真夏にはやはり、ハイパワーのエアコンをフル稼働させてしまいます。

草履
thonged straw sandals 鼻緒付きのワラのサンダル

Unlike *geta*, which are considered casual footwear, *zōri* are a type of thonged sandals chiefly made with straw or leather that tend to be worn along with traditional formal attire.

カジュアルな履物とされるげたとは異なり、草履は主にワラや革で作られた鼻緒付きのサンダルの一種で、伝統的な正装に合わせて履かれる傾向がある。

Fashion changes with the times: **thonged straw sandals** used to be paired with kimono during formal occasions, but nowadays, you're just as likely to see people sporting *zōri* while browsing a shopping arcade.

ファッションは時代とともに変化します。かつて草履は、フォーマルな場で着物に合わせるものでしたが、今では商店街でスポーツ用草履を履いている人を見かけることがよくあります。

わらじ
tie-on straw sandals 結んだワラのサンダル

Waraji are sandals made from woven rice straw.

わらじは稲ワラを編んで作ったサンダルである。

The Marathon Monks of Mt. Hiei perform feats of superhuman endurance, their soles protected by little more than **tie-on straw sandals**.

比叡山の千日回峰行僧たちは、ほぼわらじだけで足の裏を守りながら、超人的な持久力を発揮します。

帯
broad kimono sash 幅広の着物用ベルト

Traditionally a type of long, broad sash tied over kimono, modern *obi* come in a variety of shapes and sizes.

伝統的には、着物の上に結ぶ長くて幅の広いベルトの一種で、現代の帯にはさまざまな形やサイズがある。

The variety of **broad kimono sashes** and their complex knots come as a surprise to many visitors to Japan.

帯の種類の多さとその複雑な結び方に、日本を訪れる多くの人が驚きます。

地下足袋
split-toe mid-calf boots つま先の割れたふくらはぎ丈のブーツ

Jikatabi are a type of minimalist footwear featuring a split between the big toe and the rest of the toes.

地下足袋はミニマリスト向けの履物の一種で、親指部分とそれ以外の指の部分が分かれた特徴を持つ。

When Nathaniel was loaned a pair of **split-toe mid-calf boots** for the local festival, he excitedly ran around proclaiming that he was a ninja.

地元の祭りのために地下足袋を貸してもらったナサニエルは、自分は忍者だと宣言して興奮気味に走り回りました。

058

とび
high-rise construction worker 高所建設作業員

Tobi are construction workers who specialize in performing tasks on tall buildings, particularly with regard to scaffolding.

とびは、高い建物での作業を専門に行う建設作業員で、特に足場を使用する。

The image of **high-rise construction workers** wearing their ludicrously baggy pants seems at odds with a culture that tends to be risk-averse.

とびが、おかしいほどぶかぶかのズボンをはいている姿は、危険を避けようとする仕事の性質と相いれないように思えます。

腹巻き
belly wrap undergarment 腹を包む肌着

A *haramaki*, or "belly wrap," is a tube of fabric usually worn as an undergarment to keep one's midriff warm.

腹巻きとは、つまり「おなかを包むもの」のことで、通常、肌着として着用する筒状の布を指し、上腹部の保温が目的である。

Ōtani-san didn't learn to appreciate a **belly wrap undergarment** until he entered his 40s.

オオタニさんが腹巻きの良さを知ったのは、40代に入ってからでした。

暴走族
noisy biker gang 騒がしいオードバイ乗り集団

Bōsōzoku, literally translated as "running-out-of-control tribe," is a Japanese youth subculture inspired by American greaser culture.

暴走族は、直訳すると「制御不能に走り回る部族」で、アメリカのグリーサー文化に影響を受けた日本の若者サブカルチャーである。

When I lived deep in the Japanese countryside, a **noisy biker gang** would regularly parade by my apartment well past midnight, waking me from my slumber.

日本の農村部に住んでいた頃、真夜中過ぎになると暴走族が私のアパートの近くを連なって走るので、目が覚めてしまったものです。

浴衣
casual kimono bathrobe カジュアルな着物型バスローブ

Yukata, literally translated as "bathing cloth," is a summer kimono made of cotton or synthetic fabric.

浴衣は、直訳すると「水浴び用衣服」で、木綿か合成繊維で作られた夏用の着物である。

When Haru spotted Michiko at the festival wearing a colorful **casual kimono bathrobe** and a flower in her hair, his heart skipped a beat.

ハルは、カラフルな浴衣をまとい、髪に花をつけたミチコを祭りで見つけたとき、胸がときめきました。

和傘
traditional oil-paper umbrella 伝統的な油紙製傘

Wagasa, literally translated as "Japanese umbrellas," are umbrellas or parasols traditionally made of bamboo, greased paper, and string.

和傘は、直訳すると「日本の傘」で、伝統的に竹と油紙とひもで作られた雨傘または日傘である。

Though she appreciated the beauty of a **traditional oil-paper umbrella**, the only time Akiko ever actually used one was during her wedding photo shoot.

アキコは、和傘の美しさを知ってはいましたが、実際に使ったのは結婚式の写真撮影のときだけでした。

同人誌
self-published printed works
自費出版印刷作品集

Dōjinshi are self-published, printed works such as manga.
同人誌とは、漫画などを収めた自費出版の印刷物のことである。

Even though I arrived at Comiket super early in the morning, the **self-published printed works** I was after had already sold out by the time I found the writer's booth.
ずいぶん朝早くにコミケの会場に着いたにもかかわらず、目当ての同人誌は、作家のブースを見つけたときにはすでに売り切れていました。

Chapter
4

Craft/Objects
物品・工芸品

こけし

appendageless wooden doll
手脚のない木製人形

文で説明してみよう！

Kokeshi are simple wooden dolls with neither arms nor legs that are made as toys for children.

こけしは手脚のないシンプルな木製の人形で、子供のおもちゃとして作られている。

3語フレーズを会話で使おう！

The **appendageless wooden dolls** of Japan may seem simple at first glance, but their shapes and patterns are actually classified into eleven distinct types.

日本のこけしは一見シンプルですが、その形や模様は実は11種類に明確に分類されています。

Andrew's Point

I was once one of two foreigners at a small digital media company. The other foreigner loved to poke fun at people, giving them nicknames, mocking them for what he perceived as uncommon sense, and playfully imitating their quirks in his exaggerated accents. I was never really sure if he was well-liked or simply tolerated. But it was thanks to him that I learned what a *kokeshi* doll was. There was one employee at the company who had a haircut that looked just like one! Of course, she had all of her appendages, and her personality was far from wooden. But the resemblance was unmistakable.

私はかつて、小さなデジタルメディア企業に勤める2人の外国人従業員のうちの1人でした。もう一人の外国人は人をからかうのが大好きで、あだ名をつけたり、常識がないと思えばそのことをばかにしたり、大げさな口調で人の話し方の癖をものまねしたりしていました。彼が好かれているのか、単に大目に見られているのか、私にはよく分かりませんでした。でも、こけしが何なのかを知ったのは、彼のおかげです。その会社には、こけしにそっくりな髪形の従業員がいたのです！ 当然ながら、その人にはちゃんと四肢が備わっていましたし、雰囲気が堅苦しくて生気がないなどということは全くありませんでした。でも、こけしに似ていることは紛れもない事実だったのです。

こたつ

061

blanket-covered heater-affixed table

毛布で覆われたヒーター組み込み型テーブル

 文で説明してみよう！

A **kotatsu** is a low table with a built-in heater, all covered by a heavy blanket to keep people warm in the winter.

こたつはヒーターを内蔵した低いテーブルで、冬に暖かく過ごせるよう、厚手の毛布で覆われている。

 ３語フレーズを会話で使おう！

The danger of a **blanket-covered heater-affixed table** is that in no time at all, you will enter a deep slumber, becoming one with the floor.

こたつの危険性は、あっという間に深い眠りに落ちてしまい、しかも床と一体化してしまうことです。

Andrew's Point

I wanted to call this "wintertime heated bliss" because every time I tuck myself into a *kotatsu*, my body melts and I slip into a cozy, dreamy wonderland within mere minutes. But of course, that three-word phrase provides less an understanding of the object itself than it does the result. A blanket-covered heater-affixed table is dry but accurate. Now, if you explain it this way, you will undoubtedly have to add some additional details: (1) the table legs are short; (2) you sit on the ground (or on a special no-legged *kotatsu* chair); (3) it's primarily for winter. So, if I weren't limited to three words, it might sound something like "wintertime, ultra-cozy, short-legged, blanket-covered, heater-affixed table that serves as a gateway to bliss."

これはwintertime heated blissと表現したかったところです。というのも、こたつに入ると、ほんの数分で体が溶けて、居心地の良い、夢のようなワンダーランドに入り込んでしまうからです。しかしもちろん、この3語のフレーズでは、こたつに入った結果ばかりで、こたつ自体についての理解は深まりません。blanket-covered heater-affixed tableなら、味気ないけれど正確です。とはいえ、このように説明する場合、間違いなくいくつかの詳細を追加しなければならないでしょう。(1)テーブルの脚が短い、(2)床に座る（または脚のない特別なこたつ用の椅子に座る）、(3)主に冬に使われる、などです。というわけで、もし3語という縛りがなかったらwintertime, ultra-cozy, short-legged, blanket-covered, heater-affixed table that serves as a gateway to blissとしたかもしれません。

はんこ

carved signature stamp

彫り込み式署名用スタンプ

文で説明してみよう！

Hanko are uniquely carved personal stamps used in lieu of handwritten signatures for everything from receiving a delivery to signing a lease on an apartment.

はんことは、この世に１つしかない彫り込みが施されたスタンプのことで、宅配便の受け取りからアパートの賃貸契約まで、あらゆる場面で手書きの署名の代わりに使われる。

３語フレーズを会話で使おう！

No sooner did the man get a professionally made **carved signature stamp** for the express purpose of opening a new bank account than the bank upgraded to a digital signature system.

その男性が、新しい銀行口座を緊急に開設するために、プロが彫ったはんこを手に入れたとたんに、銀行はデジタル署名システムにアップグレードしました。

Andrew's Point

I was able to get by in Japan without a *hanko* for a long time. When I first arrived, I was able to find both a bank and a mobile service provider that would accept my written signature. I think it was back in 2018 or so, when I was opening a new bank account, I was told I absolutely needed one. I actually had one by that point, but I had never used it in any official capacity. About a month or two later, I had some business to take care of at the bank, and they introduced me to their new digital signature policy, eliminating the need for the *hanko*. I had gone through a significant amount of paperwork and expended a frustrating amount of time for nothing.

私は長い間、日本ではんこを持たずに生活することができました。来日当初は、銀行も携帯電話会社もサインを受け付けてくれました。2018年頃だったと思いますが、新しく銀行口座を開設する際に、はんこがどうしても必要だと言われました。実はその時点で1つ持っていたのですが、それまで公の場で使ったことはなかったのです。それから1、2カ月後、用事があって銀行に出向くと、新しい電子署名を紹介され、はんこが不要になると言われました。膨大な書類仕事をするためにストレスのたまる時間を費やしたというのに、それが無駄になったというわけです。

蚊取り線香

incense mosquito repellent
香煙蚊よけ

  文で説明してみよう！

Katorisenkō are sticks or coils of incense infused with a type of insecticide that repels or kills mosquitoes.

蚊取り線香は、蚊を撃退したり殺したりする殺虫剤を染み込ませたスティック状か渦巻き状のお香である。

  ３語フレーズを会話で使おう！

The lazy smoke wafting from the **incense mosquito repellent** kept the mosquitos at bay while we enjoyed a late summer picnic in the park.

蚊取り線香から漂うゆったりとした煙が蚊を寄せ付けず、その間、私たちは公園で晩夏のピクニックを楽しみました。

Andrew's Point

Incense is not uncommon in the West—I don't think a day went by during college when my dorm room didn't smell of lightly roasted sandalwood and lavender. So it's surprising to me that few people in the U.S. know of *katorisenkō* "mosquito coils." There are plenty of chemical "insect repellants" you can buy in the U.S., from those you spray on your body to those you spray on your clothes. But if I just want to relax in my garden, why should I go to the trouble of dousing my skin in chemicals when a pleasant-smelling *katorisenkō* does the trick?

欧米ではお香は珍しいものではありません。大学時代、寮の部屋から軽くあぶったビャクダンやラベンダーの香りがしない日はなかったと思います。ですから、アメリカで蚊取り線香を知る人がほとんどいないのは驚きです。体にスプレーするものから服に吹きかけるものまで、アメリカでは化学的な「虫よけ剤」ならいくらでも手に入ります。でも、ただ庭でくつろぎたいだけなら、心地よい香りの蚊取り線香で十分なのに、わざわざ化学物質を肌に浴びる必要があるのでしょうか。

こま犬

064

lion-dog guardian statue

獅子犬守護像

 文で説明してみよう！

Komainu are lion-like statues that guard the entrances to shrines and temples against evil spirits.

こま犬とは、神社や寺院の入り口を悪霊から守る獅子に似た像のこと。

 3語フレーズを会話で使おう！

The **lion-dog guardian statues** at my local shrine have eyes colored bright red, and I'm always afraid they're going to come alive and eat me.

地元の神社にあるこま犬は、目が明るい赤色に塗られており、息を吹き返して私を食べてしまうのではないか、といつも怖い思いをしています。

Andrew's Point

One of my favorite things about visiting Japanese shrines is the sheer variety of the *komainu*. In some cases, these statues look less like guardians than humorous caricatures. The shape, the posture, the resemblance (or not) to typical *komainu* is all up to the craftsman. If you visit the island of Tsushima, you can see several lion-dogs with balls almost as big as their bodies. They're very cute. A lion-dog at Kumano Shrine in Shirakawa City looks as if it were made by a toddler with some play-dough. I enjoy the regal statues as much as I enjoy the odder ones.

私が日本の神社を訪れる際に気に入っていることの一つが、こま犬の種類が実に多様であることです。場合によっては、守護像というよりもユーモラスな風刺画に見えるものもあります。形、姿勢、典型的なこま犬に近いか（否か）は、すべて職人次第です。対馬を訪れれば、体とほぼ同じ大きさの睾丸を持つこま犬を何体も見ることができます。とてもかわいいのです。白河市の熊野神社にあるこま犬は、幼児が粘土で作ったような感じです。私は威厳のある像も好きですが、一風変わった像も好きです。

座布団

thin floor cushion

薄い床用クッション

文で説明してみよう！

Zabuton, literally translated as "seat futon," is a thin cushion used for comfort primarily when seated on the floor.

座布団は、直訳すれば「座席の布団」で、主に床に座るときに快適でいるために使われる薄いクッションである。

３語フレーズを会話で使おう！

Kyle had no warning when Shion socked him in the face with her **thin floor cushion** after he poked fun at her low-energy karaoke performance.

カイルは、シオンのテンションの低いカラオケの歌唱をからかったせいで、全く無警戒のところをシオンに座布団でひっぱたかれてしまいました。

Andrew's Point

Recently, a certain cut of steak has been gaining popularity in the West: *zabuton* steak (also known as Denver steak). This cut of beef comes from the shoulder blade of the cow and is a highly marbled cut. Why is it called *zabuton*? Probably because it's relatively flat and rectangular. I opted not to include a shape in my three-word description because while my image of a *zabuton* is square, there are, in fact circular, rectangular, and even pentagonal ones. One thing that I wish I could have conveyed is the *zabuton*'s use in *sumō*. I love seeing the *zabuton* fly during an upset victory.

最近、欧米である種のステーキが人気を集めてきています。ザブトンステーキ（別名デンバーステーキ）です。牛の肩甲骨の部分を切り出した霜降り肉です。なぜ座布団と呼ばれるのでしょうか。おそらく比較的平らで長方形だからでしょう。私の座布団のイメージは正方形ですが、この3語フレーズに形を表す語を含めたくなかったのは、実際には円形や長方形、五角形のものまであるからです。一つ、できれば伝えたかったのが、座布団が相撲で使われていることです。私は、番狂わせのときに座布団が飛び交うさまを見るのが大好きなのです。

耳かき

066

ear wax pick

耳あかをすくい取る道具

文で説明してみよう！

A *mimikaki* is a specialized instrument used to remove ear wax.

耳かきは、耳あかの除去に特化された道具である。

3語フレーズを会話で使おう！

The idea of using an **ear wax pick** is absurd to those of European descent due to the waxier nature of their ear wax.

ヨーロッパ系の人たちの耳あかには粘り気の強い特性があるので、耳かきを使ってすくい取るという発想は不合理なのです。

Andrew's Point

"Ear wax pick" is 100% accurate, and I don't think it could be phrased any better. However, if you use this three-word expression when speaking to someone of non-Asian descent, they simply will not understand. The reason is that ear wax differs according to your DNA. Asian earwax is dry, thanks to a single-nucleotide polymorphism (SNP) in the ABCC11 gene. Non-Asian earwax is wetter, stickier, and brownish. So when a non-Asian person wants to clean out their ears, they're likely to use a cotton swab to collect it. That said, medical experts agree that it is dangerous to use cotton swabs to clean inside your ears, so proceed with caution.

ear wax pick という表現は100パーセント正確で、これ以上的確なフレーズはないと思います。しかし、アジア系ではない人たちにこの3語フレーズを使っても、簡単には理解してもらえないでしょう。なぜなら、耳あかはDNAによって違うからです。アジア人の耳あかは乾いていますが、これはABCC11遺伝子の一塩基多型（SNP）のおかげです。非アジア人の耳あかは湿り気が多く、より粘っており、茶色っぽいのです。そのため、アジア人以外の人が耳の中を掃除するときには、綿棒を使い、それに耳あかを吸着させることが多いのです。とはいえ、綿棒を使って耳の中を掃除するのは危険だというのが医療専門家たちの一致した見解なので、慎重に行いましょう。

みこし

067

portable miniature shrine

移動式小型神社

 文で説明してみよう！

A *mikoshi* is a sacred palanquin used to transport the deity of a shrine, often during a festival.

みこしとは、神社の神を運ぶための神聖なかごのことで、祭りの間に使われることが多い。

 ３語フレーズを会話で使おう！

The one time I had the opportunity to help carry a **portable miniature shrine** during a local festival, I ended up with a bruise on my shoulder the size of an orange.

一度、地元の祭りでみこしを担ぐのを手伝ったとき、肩にオレンジ大のあざができてしまいました。

Andrew's Point

I'm taking some liberties with the word "portable." According to the *Cambridge Dictionary*, portable means "light and small enough to be easily carried or moved." Compared to a typical shrine, this is accurate! But "easily" stretches the truth. I know this firsthand from the time I was invited to participate in a summertime festival in Himeji as one of the bearers of a *mikoshi*. I didn't know the rhythm or the chant or any of that, and at one point, when some people were lowering the *mikoshi*, I thought I was supposed to be raising it. I had a bump and a bruise on my shoulder for about a year as a result. But I was happy to have earned that bruise and was grateful for the opportunity.

ここでは **portable** という言葉をいくぶん柔軟に使っています。『ケンブリッジ英語辞典』によると、**portable** とは「簡単に持ち運んだり移動したりできるほど軽く小さい」という意味だそうです。いわゆる神社と比較するなら、これは間違いありません！ しかし、「簡単に」は言いすぎです。姫路の夏祭りにみこしの担ぎ手として招聘されたときに、そのことを身をもって知りました。リズムも掛け声も何も知らない私は、ある時点で、何人かがみこしを下ろそうとしているのに、持ち上げるものだと勘違いしてしまいました。その結果、肩にこぶとあざができてしまい、1年ほど消えませんでした。でも、そのあざができたことがうれしく、そのような機会に感謝しました。

風呂敷

old-fashioned wrapping cloth
旧式の包装用布

 文で説明してみよう！

Furoshiki are traditional Japanese wrapping cloths both aesthetically pleasing and versatile, often used to wrap or transport goods.

風呂敷とは、伝統的な日本の包装用布のことで、見た目にも美しく万能で、たいてい品物を包んだり運んだりするのに使われる。

 ３語フレーズを会話で使おう！

Ira once considered all the attention given to packaging in Japan excessive, but when he returned to his country, he found himself bundling his belongings in **old-fashioned wrapping cloths** on a regular basis.

アイラはかつて、日本では包装に気を使いすぎると考えていましたが、帰国してみると、自分の持ち物を風呂敷で束ねることが当たり前になっていました。

Andrew's Point

Old-fashioned might be a little misleading. After all, there are plenty of *furoshiki* with modern designs. But the concept of the wrapping cloth itself has a history of more than 1,000 years, so I felt that the description was appropriate. I am a big fan of *furoshiki*, thanks to my wife. We're a family of five, so *furoshiki* are extremely useful for separating clothes in our luggage when packing for a trip. What's strange, however, is that I've become so accustomed to using them that I'll pack a *furoshiki* in my luggage when I'm going by myself on a business trip.

old-fashioned というと少し誤解を招くかもしれません。モダンなデザインの風呂敷もたくさんありますから。でも、風呂敷というコンセプト自体には 1,000 年以上の歴史があるのですから、この表現は適切だと思いました。私は妻のおかげで風呂敷の大ファンです。わが家は 5 人家族で、風呂敷が旅行の荷造りの際、荷物の衣類を分けるのに非常に重宝しています。ところが不思議なもので、風呂敷を使い慣れると、1 人で出張に行くときにも風呂敷を荷物に入れるようになったのです。

仏壇

household family altar

家庭用一族向け祭壇

文で説明してみよう！

A *butsudan* is a small, household Buddhist family altar resembling a simple two-doored cabinet.

仏壇とは、小さな家庭用の仏式一族向け祭壇のことで、シンプルな観音開きの飾り棚に似ている。

3語フレーズを会話で使おう！

I didn't say anything when our homestay student from Austria scarfed down the orange we had placed in front of the **household family altar**—it wasn't his fault we hadn't explained the significance of the offering.

うちにホームステイしているオーストリア出身の生徒が、仏壇の前に置いたあったミカンをほおばったとき、私は何も言いませんでした──お供え物の意味を説明しなかった私たちが悪いのですから。

Andrew's Point

There are four concepts that are essential here: household, family, altar, and Buddhist. I opted to omit "Buddhist" because the word "altar" already implies something spiritual or religious, and anyone who knows anything about Japanese culture will likely be able to make the logical leap. By the way, before I ever saw a *butsudan* in real life, I saw one in a Japanese comedy. Framed in the *butsudan* was a picture of the deceased patriarch of the family. Every time something happened in the room, his expression would change in reaction. The changing of expressions in a picture is a trope I've seen in Western comedies as well, and I found it hilarious.

ここでは4つの概念が欠かせません。household（家庭）、family（一族）、altar（祭壇）、Buddist（仏教）です。Buddist は省くことにしました。というのも、altar という語に、すでに精神的、宗教的なものが含まれており、日本文化に詳しい人なら誰でも論理的にたどり着けそうだからです。ところで私は、仏壇の実物を目の当たりにする前に、日本のお笑い番組で仏壇を見ました。その仏壇には、亡くなった家長の写真が飾られていました。部屋の中で何かが起こるたびに、家長の表情が変わるのです。写真の中の人の表情が変わるというのは、欧米のコメディーでも見たことがある手法で、私は抱腹絶倒しました。

070

いろり
traditional sunken hearth
伝統的なくり抜き炉床

An **irori** is a traditional sunken hearth used for heating the home and for cooking food, and until modern times, it was considered the center of daily life in Japan.

いろりとは、暖房や調理に使われる伝統的なくり抜き炉床のことで、近代まで日本での日常生活の拠点とされていた。

I would never want a **traditional sunken hearth** of my own, but whenever I encounter one at a Japanese inn, I always feel exhilarated.

自分のいろりが欲しいと思うことはありませんが、日本の旅館に泊まっていろりがあると、いつも楽しい気分になります。

ウォシュレット
Privates-Cleansing Toilet Seat 陰部洗浄用便座

Woshuretto (a registered trademark of TOTO) is an electronic bidet toilet seat affixed in place of a standard toilet seat.

ウォシュレット（TOTOの登録商標）は、標準的な便座の代わりに取り付ける電子洗浄便座である。

Unable to read Japanese, Paul hit the wrong button on the **Privates-Cleansing Toilet Seat**, causing a jet of water to douse his scrotum.

日本語が読めないポールは、ウォシュレットのボタンを押し間違えて、噴射された水が彼の陰嚢を濡らしてしまいました。

かるた
card-based matching game 手札型の合わせゲーム

🔵 *Karuta* is a type of card game whereby players must identify and be the first to grab cards arrayed before them based on prompts read from another set of cards.

かるたはカードゲームの一種で、プレーヤーは目の前に並べられたカードを、別の山から引いたカードの指示に基づいて識別し、真っ先に取らなければならない。

💬 My oldest son, still in kindergarten, howls in dismay when he loses to me at **card-based matching game**, but I know it will only be a few more years until he regularly beats the pants off me.

私の長男はまだ幼稚園児で、かるた取りで私に負けるとがっかりして泣きわめきますが、ほんの数年のうちに常に私を打ち負かすようになることは分かっています。

けん玉
wooden skill toy 木製の技能玩具

🔵 *Kendama* is a toy that consists of a handle, a pair of cups, and a ball connected by a string, requiring the user to attempt to toss the ball and catch it in a variety of ways.

けん玉は、持ち手と一組の受け皿、玉をひもでつないだおもちゃで、さまざまな方法で玉を投げ上げ、それを受け止めることが求められる。

💬 The fine motor skills required to perform an array of **wooden skill toy** tricks are as impressive as they are elusive to me.

けん玉の技の数々をこなすのに必要な細かい運動技能は、私にとって感動的であると同時に、まず身につけられないものです。

071

だるま
perseverance-bolstering Buddhist doll
がまん強い仏教徒人形

Daruma dolls, modeled after the monk Bodhidharma, are traditional good luck charms and symbols of perseverance.

達磨大師をモデルにしただるまは、伝統的な縁起物であり、忍耐の象徴でもある。

After my friend Natalie's great-aunt passed away, she found a **perseverance-bolstering Buddhist doll** with a single eye colored in and wondered what wish had been left unfulfilled.

友人のナタリーは、大叔母が亡くなった後、片方の目だけ塗られただるまを見つけ、どんな願いがかなえられないままだったのだろうかと考えました。

なぎなた
bladed pole weapon 刃のある棒状の武器

A *naginata* is a weapon that consists of a staff with a curved single-edged blade on the end.

なぎなたは、先端に湾曲した片刃を備えた棒状の武器である。

As a former hockey player, I thought I'd strike up a conversation with the cute girl on the train holding a large stick, but when she revealed that it was actually a **bladed pole weapon**, I backed away cautiously.

元アイスホッケー選手の私は、電車の中で大きなスティックを抱えたかわいい女の子に話しかけようと思ったのですが、彼女はそれが実はなぎなただと明かしたので、私は用心して後ずさりしてしまいました。

のれん
cloth portal separator 布製の入り口仕切り

Noren are fabric dividers hung outside the entrances of shops and restaurants as well as between rooms, in doorways, and in windows.

のれんは布製の仕切りで、店やレストランの入り口の外、部屋と部屋の間、戸口や窓などに掛けられる。

Cloth portal separator may have served as an early form of climate control, but now they function as both simple partition and decoration alike.

のれんは、昔は温度調節の役割を担う道具だったかもしれませんが、今では単純な間仕切りとしても装飾としても機能しています。

らでん
shell inlay technique 貝殻象眼技法

Raden is a decorative technique whereby mother-of-pearl and other types of seashells are thinly shaved and inlaid in lacquerware and woodwork.

らでんは、真珠貝などの貝殻を薄く削り、漆器や木工品にはめ込む装飾技法である。

Ami marveled at the jewelry box, noting how the shell inlay technique created intricate patterns that shimmered in the light.

アミはその宝石箱を見て驚嘆しました。らでんが作り出す複雑な模様が、光を受けてきらめいて見えたからです。

火鉢
traditional charcoal-burning brazier
伝統的な炭焼き鉢

072

📄 A *hibachi*, literally translated as "fire bowl," is an open-topped brazier designed to burn charcoal or wood for cooking.

火鉢は、直訳すると「火のボウル」で、炭や薪を燃やして調理するために設計された上部開放型の鉢である。

💬 There are many **traditional charcoal-burning brazier** restaurants in the U.S. that actually grill their food using *teppan*, which are flat, iron grills.

アメリカには、火鉢レストランがたくさんあり、実際には平たい鉄板を使って食材を焼いています。

割り箸
disposable wooden chopsticks 使い捨て木製箸

📄 *Waribashi*, literally translated as "break chopsticks," are disposable chopsticks made of wood or bamboo that must be pulled apart before being used.

割り箸は、直訳すると「箸を割る」で、使う前に引き離す必要のある木製または竹製の箸である。

💬 Whenever we order delivery, the food comes with **disposable wooden chopsticks**, but we always use our own chopsticks, so we have a massive bundle of chopsticks stuffed in the back of a drawer that we don't know what to do with.

出前を頼むと必ず割り箸が付いてくるのですが、私たちはいつも自分たちの箸を使うので、引き出しの奥にどうすればいいのか分からないほど大量の箸の束が詰まっています。

座椅子
legless floor chair 脚のない床置き椅子

Zaisu, literally translated as "seating chair," is a legless chair with a sturdy back right atop the floor, often found in *tatami* rooms.

座椅子は、直訳すると「座るための椅子」で、脚のない背もたれが頑丈な椅子であり、たいてい畳の部屋に置かれる。

The older I get, the more I appreciate the back support provided by a **legless floor chair**.

年を取れば取るほど、座椅子が背中を支えてくれることがありがたくなるのです。

手ぬぐい
cotton hand towel 木綿のハンドタオル

Tenugui are thin cotton hand towels often featuring a colorful, hand-dyed pattern.

手ぬぐいは薄い木綿のハンドタオルで、たいていカラフルな手染め模様が特徴である。

When I visited my Australian host family ten years after I returned to Japan, I was surprised to see the **cotton hand towel** I had given them framed on a wall in their foyer.

日本に帰国して10年後にオーストラリアのホストファミリーを訪ねたら、驚いたことに、私が贈った手ぬぐいが玄関の壁に額装されていました。

床の間
aesthetic display alcove 美的展示用壁のくぼみ

073

Tokonoma is a raised alcove in a room reserved for items of artistic appreciation, such as hanging scrolls, pottery, and flower arrangements.

床の間とは、部屋の中の一段高いくぼんだスペースのことで、掛け軸や陶器、生け花など、芸術的な鑑賞品を置くために設けられている。

The first thing Kimihiko did when he entered his family's room at the inn was to remove the pottery from the **aesthetic display alcove**; he knew that his two-year-old daughter would otherwise climb up and wreak havoc as soon as he looked away.

キミヒコが、旅館で自分たち家族の泊まる部屋に入って最初にしたことは、床の間の壺をどけることでした。そうしないと、目を離したすきに彼の2歳の娘がはい上がってめちゃくちゃにするでしょうから。

招き猫
waving cat figure 手を振るネコの像

Manekineko, literally translated as "beckoning cat," are cat figurines with one paw held up as if waving or beckoning, and they are believed to bring good luck to their owners.

招き猫は、直訳すると「手招きするネコ」で、片方の前足を振るか手招きするかのように上げたネコの置き物のことであり、持ち主に幸運をもたらすと信じられている。

Christian's **waving cat figure**, his most treasured souvenir from his trip to Japan, waved to him from his living room window as if welcoming him home from work.

クリスチャンの招き猫は、彼が日本への旅行から持ち帰った一番大切な土産で、まるで仕事から帰宅した彼を歓迎しているかのように居間の窓から手を振っていました。

障子
translucent room divider 半透明の間仕切り

🔵 **Shōji** are doors, windows, and room dividers made of thick, translucent paper stretched over a lattice frame of wood or bamboo.

障子とは、木や竹で組まれた格子状の枠に、厚手の半透明の紙を張った戸や窓、間仕切りのことである。

💬 I asked my grandfather why his **translucent room divider** was missing its paper, and he sighed and said simply, "Cats and *shoji* do not mix."

祖父に、なぜ障子紙がはがれているのかと尋ねると、祖父はため息をついて一言「ネコと障子は相いれないな」と言いました。

畳
comfy rush flooring 快適なイグサの床

🔵 **Tatami** is a thick, woven straw mat traditionally made from common rush or soft rush.

畳は、伝統的にイグサで作られた厚手の織りわらのマットである。

💬 The moment I entered the Japanese inn, I was struck by the smell of old, **comfy rush flooring**, immediately transporting me back to my youth in the countryside.

旅館に入った瞬間、私は古い畳の匂いに心を打たれ、即座に田舎で過ごした若い頃のことがよみがえってきました。

埴輪
terracotta clay figure 赤褐色の粘土像

074

📄 *Haniwa*, literally translated as "clay ring," are unglazed terracotta rings, cylinders, and figures that served as funerary objects as early as the late third century A.D.

埴輪は、直訳すると「粘土の輪」で、紀元3世紀後半という古い時代に葬送品として使用された素焼きの赤褐色の輪や円筒、人形のことである。

💬 While we have some ideas concerning how **terracotta clay figures** were used, we can only speculate about how people considered them in ancient times.

埴輪がどのように使われていたかについては、ある程度の見当はつきますが、古代の人々が埴輪をどのように考えていたかについては、推測するしかありません。

生け花
classical flower arrangement
古典的なフラワーアレンジメント

📄 *Ikebana*, literally translated as "letting flowers live," is the art of creating floral arrangements with blossoms, branches, leaves, and stems according to a specific set of rules that govern their form.

生け花は、直訳すると「花を生かすこと」であり、花や枝、葉、茎を使って、形態を規定する一定のルールに沿った植物のアレンジメントを創作する芸術である。

💬 Harrison could see that the **classical flower arrangements** at the exhibition were imbued with a structured sort of dynamism, but he knew that without serious study, it was something he would never be able to replicate himself.

ハリソンは、展示会の生け花が構造化されたある種のダイナミズムを帯びていることは分かりましたが、真剣に勉強しない限り、自分では決して再現できないものだと思いました。

すごろく
Snakes and Ladders ヘビとはしご

Sugoroku, literally translated as "double sixes," is a board game akin to Snakes and Ladders, often played by children over the New Year's holiday.

すごろくは、直訳すると「2つの6」で、正月休みに子供たちがよく遊ぶ、「ヘビとはしご」に似たボードゲームである。

As soon as *Kimetsu No Yaiba* surged in popularity, sure enough, a new themed **Snakes and Ladders** board followed.

『鬼滅の刃』の人気が急上昇すると、案の定、それをモチーフにした新しいすごろくが出てきました。

ちょうちん
traditional paper lantern 伝統的な紙張り手提げランプ

Chōchin are traditional Japanese lanterns made by gluing Japanese paper, or *washi*, to frames of thin bamboo hoops.

ちょうちんは、日本の伝統的な手提げランプで、細い竹の輪の枠に和紙をのり付けして作られる。

The alley was silent and shrouded in darkness, save for a lone alcove brushed with the red of a dimly lit **traditional paper lanterns**.

ぽつんと離れたあずまやが薄暗いちょうちんの赤い光に照らされている以外、路地は静かで闇に包まれていました。

布団
quilted sleeping pad キルト風睡眠用詰め物

075

A *futon* is a traditional style of bedding whereby a stuffed, quilted sleeping pad sits directly on the floor or atop a mat.

布団は寝具の伝統的な様式の一つで、床やマットの上に直接置く、詰め物をしたキルティングの睡眠用パッドである。

The *eikaiwa* school that employed me promised a fully furnished apartment, but when I first walked in and discovered a simple **quilted sleeping pad** on the tatami floor, I couldn't help but be a little surprised—although I soon learned to love it.

私を雇ってくれた英会話学校は、家具付きのアパートの手配を約束してくれたのですが、初めて部屋に入って畳の上に簡素な布団が敷いてあるのを見たときは、少し驚かずにはいられませんでした──もっとも、すぐにそれも大好きになりましたが。

浮世絵
Edo woodblock print 江戸時代の木版画

Ukiyo-e are woodblock prints and paintings made during the Edo period.

浮世絵とは、江戸時代に制作された木版画や絵画のことである。

While Hokusai's most reputed work may be his **Edo woodblock print** The Great Wave off Kanagawa, I'm more partial to his painting Aka Shōki.

北斎の最も有名な作品は浮世絵の「神奈川沖浪裏」かもしれませんが、私は「赤鍾馗」をもっと偏愛しています。

風鈴
summertime wind bell 夏季の風鈴

Fūrin are small Japanese "wind bells" or chimes, often hung from the eaves of a house.

風鈴は小型の日本の「風鈴」つまりチャイムで、たいてい家の軒先につるされる。

The oppressive summer heat robbed the day of its energy, the only protest lodged by the faint ringing of a solitary **summertime wind bell**.

夏の厳しい暑さが一日の活力を奪ってしまい、唯一それにあらがうのは、たった一つの風鈴が鳴るかすかな音でした。

輪島塗り
Wajima-style traditional lacquerware
輪島流の伝統的な漆器

Wajimanuri is a type of lacquerware made by applying multiple layers of lacquer mixed with powdered diatomaceous earth found only in the city of Wajima, Ishikawa Prefecture.

輪島塗りは、石川県輪島市のみで見られる、粉末状の珪藻土を混ぜた漆を何層にも塗り重ねたタイプの漆器である。

I brought my Scottish friend some **Wajima-style traditional lacquerware** bowls, but instead of using them for soup as I expected, she placed them in her breakfront with her other cherished items.

私はスコットランド人の友人のところに輪島塗りのお椀を持って行ったのですが、彼女は私の期待に反してスープ用の器としては使わず、他の大切な品々と一緒に戸棚に飾りました。

076

木魚
slit fish drum 切り込み入り魚太鼓

📝 *Mokugyo* are eyeless, fish-shaped drums struck to accompany the chanting of sutras.

木魚とは、目のない魚の形の太鼓のことで、読経に合わせて打ち鳴らされる。

💬 The hypnotic sound of the **slit fish drum** primed my mind to receive the sutras.

催眠術のような木魚の音が、私の心にお経を受け入れるよう促してくれました。

路線図
railway transit map 鉄道乗り換え地図

📝 *Rosenzu* are transit maps.

路線図とは乗り換え用地図のこと。

💬 If it weren't for the **railway transit map**, Alex would have gotten completely and utterly lost in the tangled mess of train lines.

もし路線図がなかったら、アレックスは複雑に入り組んだ鉄道路線につかまり、すっかり迷子になっていたでしょう。

Chapter
5

Sociology/Philosophy
社会制度・思想

かんちょう

butthole poke prank
肛門つつきの悪ふざけ

  文で説明してみよう！

Kanchō, literally translated as "enema," is a prank performed by interlocking one's fingers and extending the pointer fingers in the shape of an imaginary gun, followed by attempting to poke an unsuspecting victim in the anus.

かんちょうは、字義どおりにはenema（浣腸）のことだが、ここでは複数本の指を組み、銃を思わせる形に両人差し指を伸ばして、無防備な被害者の肛門を突こうとする悪ふざけである。

  ３語フレーズを会話で使おう！

For many foreigners who come to teach English at middle schools in Japan, a **butthole poke prank** from one of their students is something of a rite of passage.

日本の中学校に英語を教えに来る多くの外国人にとって、生徒からの「かんちょう」は通過儀礼のようなものです。

Andrew's Point

Let me make something clear from the start: I do not condone *kanchō*. In many countries, it would be considered outright sexual assault, and perpetrators could be strictly disciplined or jailed. That said, when I encountered the term in a blog back in 2004, I thought it was one of the funniest things I had ever read. A teacher at a junior high school remarked how seemingly sweet little girls would lower your defenses and then turn into *kanchō* assassins the second you turned away. I've been fortunate never to have been a *kanchō* victim.

まず、はっきりさせておきたいことがあります。私はかんちょうを容認しません。多くの国で、これは明白な性的暴行と見なされ、加害者は厳しく処分されたり投獄されたりする可能性があります。とはいえ、2004年に、とあるブログでこの言葉に出くわしたとき、今まで読んだ中で最も面白いものの一つだと思いました。ある中学校の教員が書いたものです。一見かわいらしい少女たちが、どうやって人に警戒心を解かせ、背を向けた瞬間にかんちょうの刺客に変貌するかについて述べてありました。私は幸い、かんちょうの犠牲者になったことは一度もありません。

敬語

nuanced layered politeness
微妙な多重層の丁寧さ

文で説明してみよう！

Keigo is the Japanese system of honorific speech used to convey respect.

敬語とは、敬意を伝えるために使われる日本の尊敬話法の体系のこと。

３語フレーズを会話で使おう！

I was, at first, opposed to the idea of **nuanced layered politeness**—as an American, I reject the idea of considering people "above" or "below" me.

私は当初、敬語の考え方に反対でした——私はアメリカ人なので、人に「上」「下」があるとする発想を受け入れられないのです。

Andrew's Point

The hardest part of coming up with a three-word expression for "keigo" is trying to differentiate it from other languages that have polite speech forms. For example, in Spanish, you address people differently if they're a friend or someone you're not well-acquainted with. At first, I came up with "polite, respectful language," and I thought "respectful" helped to emphasize the "son-" in "sonkeigo." But that expression also applies to many other languages. To make the phrase more distinctly Japanese (without, of course, using the word "Japanese,"), I settled on "nuanced layered politeness." In my experience, there are layers of politeness that are expressed in subtle, nuanced ways, sometimes difficult even for native Japanese speakers to grasp.

「敬語」の3語フレーズを考える上で一番難しいのは、丁寧な形式ををを持つ他の言語とどう区別すればいいかです。例えば、スペイン語では、相手が友人か、あまり親しくない人かによって呼び方を変えます。最初に思いついたのは、**polite, respectful language** でした。そして、**respectful** は「尊敬語」の「尊」強調するのに役立つと考えました。しかし、この表現は他の多くの言語にも当てはまってしまいます。そこで、フレーズをより明確に日本語寄りのものにするために(もちろん **Japanese** という語を使わずに)、**nuanced layered politeness** という表現に決めました。私の経験では、非常に微妙な形で表現される丁寧さの複数の層があり、それは日本語を母語とする人でさえ時に理解するのが難しいものです。

引きこもり

socially withdrawn shut-in

社会的に交流を持たずに閉じこもった人

 文で説明してみよう！

Hikikomori are recluses who eschew social contact, often keeping to their homes for months or years at a time.

ひきこもりは、社会との接触を避ける世捨て人で、一度に数カ月から数年間家に閉じこもることが多い。

 3語フレーズを会話で使おう！

Although our friend occasionally posted memes to social media, we hadn't seen her in so long that we were afraid she had become a **socially withdrawn shut-in**.

友人はときどきSNSにミームを投稿していましたが、私たちはずいぶん長い間その友人に会っていなかったので、彼女が引きこもりになってしまったのではないかと心配しました。

Andrew's Point

One of the many negative outcomes of the COVID-19 pandemic was an increase in *hikikomori*. But the phenomenon was not just isolated in Japan, with its 1.5 million sufferers (as of mid-2023, up from around 1.2 million pre-COVID). Indeed, studies have identified *hikikomori* everywhere, from Hong Kong to Spain to the U.S. to Nigeria. And the term itself is showing up more frequently these days in research papers and news articles. It is my hope that as social media evolves to become more empathetically designed and community-focused, it will play a significant role in alleviating rather than exacerbating the *hikikomori* condition.

新型コロナウイルス感染症の大流行がもたらした多くの悪影響の一つは、引きこもりの増加でした。しかし、この現象は150万人（2023年半ば現在、コロナ以前の約120万人から増加）の引きこもりを抱える日本だけのものではありません。実際、香港、スペイン、アメリカ、ナイジェリアなど、あらゆる場所で引きこもりが確認されています。この言葉自体も、最近では研究論文やニュース記事で頻繁に目にするようになりました。私の望みは、SNSがより共感を呼ぶように設計され、地域社会に焦点を当てたものへと進化するにつれて、引きこもりの状態を悪化させるのではなく改善するために、重要な役割を果たすようになることです。

甘え

080

dependent emotional closeness

依存型の感情的親密さ

文で説明してみよう！

Amae is a term expressing a deep, ingrained aspect of Japanese interpersonal relations, capturing the sense of a person behaving in a dependent or "child-like" manner, expecting indulgence and indulging others.

甘えは、日本人の対人関係の奥深くに根付いているものを表す言葉で、依存的な、あるいは「子供じみた」振る舞いをすることによって、他人から大目に見てもらうことを期待する感覚を捉えたものである。

３語フレーズを会話で使おう！

In a heated conversation, the mother reprimanded her son for his **dependent emotional closeness**, telling him that he needs to learn to handle his problems independently instead of always relying on her to solve them.

激しい口論の中で、母は息子の甘えを叱責し、いつも母親頼みで問題を解決しようとせずに、自分で対処することを覚えなければだめだと言いました。

Andrew's Point

The first few times I encountered "amae" in Japan was in the context of *amaenbō*, so I believed the term to be equivalent to "spoiled child" in English. But over time, I realized that it has a much deeper cultural aspect, manifesting not only in parent-child relationships but also between spouses, friends, and colleagues. While there is a sort of neediness or dependence to it, it's a part of a framework of mutual understanding, trust, and emotional bonding. "Spoiled" conveys none of these positive aspects, so I felt it wasn't appropriate despite being related.

日本で初めて「甘え」という言葉に遭遇したのはのは甘えん坊に関する話の中だったので、てっきり英語で言う spoiled child（甘やかされた子供）に相当するものだとそのとき思ってしまいました。しかし、時がたつにつれて、これにはもっと深い文化的側面があり、親子関係だけでなく、夫婦間や友人同士、同僚同士にもあるものであることに気がついたのです。ある種の相手を必要とする気持ちや相手に依存する気持ちがある一方で、相互理解や信頼、感情的なきずなを形作るものの一部なのです。spoiled は、そのようなポジティブな側面をまったく感じさせない言葉なので、関連はするけれどここで使うには不適切だと感じました。

義理と人情

love and duty

愛情と義務感

 文で説明してみよう！

The concept of *giri to ninjō* represents the conflict between *giri*, the obligation to act according to societal conventions in relation to other people, and *ninjō*, the human emotions that may compel a person to do otherwise.

義理と人情の概念は、他者との関係において社会の慣習に従って行動する義務としての義理と、そうでない行動をとらざるを得ない人間の感情としての人情との間の葛藤を表すものである。

 ３語フレーズを会話で使おう！

The older I get, the more I worry that young people are unable to strike a proper balance between **love and duty**.

年を取るほどに、若い人たちが義理と人情の適切なバランスを取れないのではないかと心配になります。

Andrew's Point

"Love and duty" aligns closely with "giri to ninjō" because it delineates the contrast between societal obligations and personal feelings. "Duty" corresponds to *giri*, indicating unwavering allegiance to societal norms and familial commitments, whereas terms like "commitment" or "allegiance" alone could misrepresent the inherent selflessness and sacrifice. Conversely, "love" mirrors *ninjō*, reflecting inherent warmth and emotional connections, something terms like "emotion" or "feeling" can't fully encompass due to their broadness and lack of specificity to positive affection.

love and duty は、社会的な義務と個人的な感情との対比を表しているので、「義理と人情」とピッタリ呼応しています。**duty** は義理に対応し、社会規範や家族への揺るぎない忠誠を表します。一方、**commitment** や **allegiance** だと、単独では変に無私無欲や犠牲のニュアンスが伝わってしまいます。逆に **love** は人情を反映した言葉で、温かさや感情的なつながりといったニュアンスが伝わります。そうしたニュアンスは **emotion** や **feeling** では表現しきれないものです。なぜなら、意味の範囲が広すぎて、ポジティブな好感に特化できないからです。

婚活

formal spouse-hunting activity

正式な配偶者探し活動

 文で説明してみよう！

Konkatsu, a portmanteau of "kekkon" and "katsudō," are social events specifically geared toward helping people find a life partner.

婚活とは、「結婚」と「活動」の合成語で、人生のパートナー探しにつなげることに特化した社交の機会のこと。

 ３語フレーズを会話で使おう！

If you know of any well-to-do single men in their thirties, please let me know, as my sister-in-law is currently engaged in **formal spouse-hunting activities**.

30代の裕福な独身男性を知っていたら、教えてください。義理の妹が婚活中なのです。

Andrew's Point

That the term *konkatsu* exists at all implies that there's a distinct formality and organization to it, which is why I felt the word "formal" was essential. Spouse-hunting activities exist in the U.S., but they're much more casual. People might look for potential spouses through informal social networks or online platforms—the use of agencies fell out of fashion decades ago. And while there are certainly singles events in the U.S., they're not explicitly for the sake of finding a marriage partner as they are in Japan. American singles events are generally more casual and are aimed at meeting new people for a range of relationship types, from friendships to casual dating to potential long-term relationships. While some participants may have marriage in mind, it's usually not the stated goal of these events.

婚活という言葉が存在するということは、それなりの正式な手続きや段取りがあることが示唆されます。だから私は、**formal**という語が欠かせないと感じたのです。配偶者探しの活動はアメリカにもありますが、はるかにカジュアルなものです。気軽なソーシャルネットワークやオンラインプラットフォームを通じて配偶者候補を探すことは、あるかもしれません。また、アメリカにも独身者向けのイベントはありますが、日本のように明確に結婚相手を探すためのものではありません。アメリカの独身者向けイベントは、概してもっとカジュアルで、友人関係からカジュアルなデート、長期的に発展するかもしれない交際まで、さまざまなタイプの人間関係を築くための新しい出会いを目的としています。参加者の中には結婚を意識している人もいますが、通常は結婚が目的ではありません。

遅延証明書

train delay certificate
列車の遅延証明書

文で説明してみよう！

A *chien shōmeisho* is a certificate that passengers can obtain from station staff after a delay due to an accident or inclement weather to show to a boss, teacher, or the like the reason for their lateness.

遅延証明書とは、事故や悪天候で列車の運行が遅れた場合に、乗客が駅員からもらう証明書のことで、上司や教員などに遅刻の理由を示すために使われる。

3語フレーズを会話で使おう！

Without a **train delay certificate**, I'll be screwed: I've already been late to the restaurant twice this week, so I'm sure to lose my job.

遅延証明書がないとまずいことになります。 今週はすでに2回も遅刻してしいるので、絶対にクビになるでしょう。

Andrew's Point

The idea of a train delay certificate may sound absurd to people in the U.S., where on some lines train delays are considered the norm rather than the exception. But if you mention the concept to a German, they'll likely tell you about their own: the *Bescheinigung über Zugverspätung*. Indeed, there are a handful of places that offer similar certificates, including lines in Belgium, Hong Kong, and the Netherlands. And in the U.K., if your train is delayed by more than 15 or 30 minutes (depending on the line), you can request repayment of 50% of your ticket price.

遅延証明書というものを作ろうという発想は、一部の路線では列車の遅延など当たり前で特別なことではないと考えられているアメリカに暮らす人たちには、ばかばかしく聞こえるかもしれません。しかし、ドイツ人にこのコンセプトについて話せば、ドイツ独自の **Bescheinigung über Zugverspätung**（列車遅延証明書）について教えてくれるでしょう。実際、ベルギー、香港、オランダなど、同じような証明書を発行しているところはいくつかあります。またイギリスでは、電車が15分から30分（路線によって異なる）を超えて遅れた場合、運賃の50パーセントの返済を求めることができます。

定年

084

mandatory retirement age
強制的退職年齢

 文で説明してみよう！

Teinen is the mandatory retirement age in Japan, legally fixed at 65 as of 2020, though there are exceptions in a variety of industries.

定年とは日本における強制的退職年齢のことで、法的には2020年現在、65歳と定められているが、さまざまな業界で例外がある。

 ３語フレーズを会話で使おう！

I'm worried that once my workaholic father reaches **mandatory retirement age**, he won't know what to do with all of his new free time.

心配なのは、仕事中毒の父が定年を迎えたら、新たに手に入る自由時間を何に使えばいいのか分からなくなるのではないかということです。

Andrew's Point

A mandatory retirement age is illegal in the U.S. except in a few cases, two of which are pilots at 65, and air traffic controllers at 56 with exceptions up to 61 (interestingly, air traffic controllers also have a maximum hiring age: 31, with exceptions up to 36 for those with experience). I appreciate that the law is working to keep planes safely up in the air. Unfortunately, the current state of the U.S. is such that many people cannot afford to retire at all. Rising living costs, unaffordable healthcare, stagnant wages, and inadequate pensions are pushing older citizens to continue working.

アメリカでは定年制は違法ですが、いくつか例外があります。そのうちの2つが、パイロットの65歳定年と航空管制官の56歳定年（特別に61歳定年も）です（興味深いことに、航空管制官には採用年齢の上限も設けられています）。飛行機を安全に空に飛ばすために法律が機能していることは評価できます。あいにく、アメリカの現状では、多くの人が、退職してしまうと暮らせなくなります。高騰する生活費、手の届かない医療、低迷する賃金、不十分な年金などが、高齢者に働き続けることを迫っているのです。

年功序列

age-based promotion system

年齢に基づく昇進昇給制度

文で説明してみよう！

Nenkōjoretsu is a seniority-wage system whereby the position and pay of a company's employees are determined by their proximity to retirement.

年功序列とは、年齢ベースの給与制度で、定年が近いかどうかで従業員の役職や賃金が決まる。

３語フレーズを会話で使おう！

In many Western cultures, employees' compensation is tied directly to their ability to contribute to the company's bottom line, so an **age-based promotion system** would never fly.

多くの西洋文化圏では、従業員の報酬は会社の収益に貢献する能力に直接結び付いているので、年功序列は決して成り立たないでしょう。

Andrew's Point

Age-based promotion systems have become obsolete in the U.S. largely due to shifts in employment practices and the rise of industries like tech, where merit and innovation are held in higher regard. The influence of Silicon Valley, known for valuing skills and results over age, has played a significant role in this transition, promoting a culture where professional advancement is based on achievement and competence rather than seniority. This shift is aligned with broader societal moves toward equality and meritocracy in professional settings. Additionally, in the UK, such age-based systems are illegal under the Equality Act 2010, reinforcing a global trend toward equitable and performance-based advancement.

米国では、年功序列は廃れてきています。主な理由は、雇用慣行の変化や、実力とイノベーションを優先するハイテク産業の台頭です。年齢よりも技能や成果を評価することで知られるシリコンバレーの影響は、この変化に大きな役割を果たし、年齢よりも実績や能力に基づいて昇進する文化を促進しました。この転換は、専門職における平等と実力主義を目指す、より広範な社会の動きに呼応しています。加えて、イギリスでは、2010年の平等法に基づいて、こうした年齢に基づいた制度は違法とされており、公平で成果に基づいた昇進・昇給を目指す世界的な傾向を後押ししています。

本音と建前

honesty facade duality
正直に見せかけた二面性

文で説明してみよう！

Honne to tatemae describes the tension that exists between a person's true feelings (*honne*) and the facade (*tatemae*) shown in public.

本音と建前は、人の本心（本音）と人前での見せかけ（建前）の間にある綱引き状態を表す。

３語フレーズを会話で使おう！

While **honesty facade duality** serves to preserve harmony in Japanese culture, it can sow discord in other countries when it's considered dishonest and insincere.

日本の文化では、本音と建前は調和を保つことに役立ちますが、他の国では不正直で不誠実だと見なされると、いざこざを招きかねません。

Andrew's Point

This one was tough to compress. I used "honesty" as a substitute for "honest feelings." They're not the same—honesty has a set of broader meanings—but they're close enough. I also could have gone with "truth" as a substitute for "true feelings," but I felt that "honesty" was closer to the heart. Meanwhile, "facade" is close enough to "public facade." As a foreigner, "hone to tatemae" is one of the cultural aspects I had a lot of trouble with when I first arrived in Japan. I accidentally offended and upset a lot of people unintentionally. I hope that in seventeen years in Japan, I've learned to do that less often—or at least less often unintentionally.

これはフレーズに圧縮するのが大変でした。honesty を honest feelings（正直な気持ち）の代わりに使いました。この2つは同じではありません——honesty のほうが広い意味を表します——が、大差はありません。truth を true feelings の代わりに使うことも考えたのですが、honesty のほうがより核心に近いと思ったのです。一方、facade は public facade（表向き）とほぼ同じです。本音と建前は、外国人である私が来日当初に苦労した文化的側面の一つです。私は意図せずして多くの人を不快にさせ、怒らせてしまいました。日本に暮らした17年間で、そのようなことが少なくなるように——いや、少なくとも意図せずして少なくなるように学んできていればいいのですが。

087

けじめ
making transitional distinctions
変化に区別をつけること

Kejime is correctly identifying and responding to changing contexts.

けじめは、変化する状況を正しくくみ取り、それに対応することである。

Some say that the foundations of **making transitional distinctions** are taught as early as kindergarten, where young children learn to recognize and shift gears in accordance with the different activities of the day.

けじめの基礎は、幼稚園に通うほど早い段階で教え込まれるものだと言う人もいます。幼い子どもたちは、一日のさまざまな活動を区別し、対応を切り替えることを学ぶのです。

ゴールデンウイーク
springtime consecutive holidays 春季の連休

Gōrudenuīku, or "golden week," is the series of four national holidays that occur within the span of a week between the end of April and the beginning of May each year.

ゴールデンウィーク、つまり「黄金週間」とは、毎年4月末から5月上旬にかけての1週間に続く4日分の祝日のことである。

Many worried that the **springtime consecutive holidays** would bring with them a new surge in cases of COVID-19.

多くの人々が、ゴールデンウイークで新型コロナウイルスの感染者が急増するのではないかと心配しました。

神道
Indigenous Animistic Religion 土着の精霊崇拝宗教

Shintō, literally translated as "the way of the gods," is the indigenous, polytheistic religion of Japan that holds that all things are imbued with supernatural entities.

神道は、直訳すると「神々の道」で、万物に超自然的な存在が宿っていると考える日本固有の多神教である。

Indigenous Animistic Religion and Buddhism may play prominent roles in Japanese culture and discourse, but the populace is, for the most part, rather secular.

神道や仏教は日本の文化や言説の中で重要な役割を果たしているかもしれませんが、一般の国民はたいてい、宗教とは無縁です。

ご縁
predestined personal affinity
運命づけられた個人的な相性

Goen describes the predestined personal affinity to people and other things.

ご縁とは、人や他のものに対する、運命づけられた個人的な相性のことである。

It must have been some sort of **predestined personal affinity** when, late at night in Kyoto, riding aimlessly on a bike after a party gone awry, I called out to some strangers frolicking in front of a karaoke joint and they ultimately became my close friends.

あれはある意味で、ご縁だったにちがいありません。京都で深夜、宴会が盛り上がった後、自転車であてもなく走っていたとき、カラオケ店の前ではしゃいでいた見知らぬ人たちに声をかけたら、結果的にその人たちと親しくなったのですから。

088

わび・さび
beauty of imperfection 不完全の美学

📄 *Wabi-sabi* is a philosophy that promotes the appreciation of the ephemeral and imperfect.

わび・さびは、はかないものや不完全なものを大切にする哲学である。

💬 **Beauty of imperfection** is most easily exemplified by a simple rock garden.

わび・さびの最も良い例は、シンプルな
石庭です。

飲みニケーション
communication through drinking 飲酒を通じた意思疎通

📄 *Nominikēshon*, a portmanteau of "nomi" and "communication," is the idea of using alcohol as a social lubricant to encourage more open communication.

飲みニケーションは、「飲み」とcommunicationの合成語で、より開放的
な対人関係を促進するためにアルコールを付き合いの潤滑油として使おう
という考え方である。

💬 In the Shōwa period, **communication through drinking** was a commonplace after-hours work activity, but these days, young office workers often go out of their way to avoid such engagements.

昭和の時代には、飲みニケーションは当たり前の就業時間外労働の一つでしたが、
最近の若い勤め人は、その手の拘束から逃れようとすることが多くなっています。

けんか両成敗
equal blame resolution 平等に非があるという解決

🔵 *Kenkaryōseibai* is the principle that both parties in a quarrel should be equally punished, regardless of the circumstances.

けんか両成敗とは、けんかの当事者はどんな状況であろうと等しく罰せられるべきだという原則である。

💬 When two students were caught in a heated argument over a misplaced lunchbox, the teacher decided to implement **equal blame resolution**, giving them both detention.

私が日本での運転を拒否する理由のひとつは、ケンカリョウセイバイのせいで、事故の際、厳密には私に過失がなくても、法律上は私に一部過失があるとみなされる可能性があるからだ。

バブル景気
late-1980s economic bubble 1980年代後半の経済バブル

🔵 *Baburu keiki* was an economic bubble that occurred from 1986 to 1991 in which real estate and stock market prices were greatly inflated.

バブル景気とは、1986年から1991年にかけて不動産価格や株価が大幅に高騰した経済バブルのことである。

💬 During the height of the **late-1980s economic bubble**, international tourists from Japan bought everything from luxury handbags to New York's Rockefeller Center.

バブル景気の全盛期、日本の観光客は海外で、高級ハンドバッグからニューヨークのロックフェラーセンターまで、あらゆるものを買いあさりました。

089

戸籍
official family register 公式の家族登録

A *koseki* is an official document that records and certifies the personal events that occur in a person's life, including birth, childbirth, marriage, and death.

戸籍は、出生、出産、婚姻、死亡といった人の一生に起こる個人的な出来事を記録し、証明する公文書である。

Fortunately, after moving from Kyoto to Nara, I was able to get copies of my **official family register** by mail and not have to go all the way back to the Kyoto ward office.

幸いなことに、京都から奈良に引っ越した後、戸籍謄本を郵送してもらえたので、わざわざ京都の区役所に再度出向かなくて済みました。

根回し
systematic back-channel consensus-building
組織的な裏ルートの合意形成

Nemawashi, literally translated as "going around the roots," is an informal process of laying the foundation for a change or proposal by building consensus among decision-makers one person at a time.

根回しは、直訳すると「根の周りを回ること」で、変更や提案の基礎を築く非公式なプロセスである。意思決定者間で、個別に合意を取る。

We might have gotten the upper hand on our foreign competitors if not for the time it took for comprehensive **systematic back-channel consensus-building**.

全員に根回しするのにかかったあの時間がなければ、海外の競合他社より優位に立てたかもしれません。

失われた10年
economically stagnant decade 経済的に停滞した10年間

Ushinawareta jūnen is the period of economic stagnation after Japan's bubble economy imploded toward the end of 1991.

失われた10年とは、1991年末にかけて日本でバブル経済が崩壊した後、経済が停滞した期間のことである。

One might expect that the inactivity of the **economically stagnant decade** would be accompanied by a decline in the personal well-being of the masses, but during that time, thanks in part to government support, well-being actually improved.

失われた10年の停滞状況が、一般庶民の個人的な幸福度の低下につながるだろうと予想する人もいたかもしれませんが、この間、政府の支援もあって、実際には幸福度は向上したのです。

終身雇用制
lifetime employment system 生涯にわたる雇用制度

Largely a relic of the 20th century, Japan's *shūshin koyōsei* has hired and trained employees straight out of school and supported them with a variety of services up until retirement.

ほとんど20世紀の遺物である日本の終身雇用制は、学校を卒業してすぐに従業員を雇用・研修し、定年退職までさまざまな福利厚生でサポートしてきた。

The decline of the **lifetime employment system** in recent years has led to a more dynamic but less predictable job market in Japan.

近年、終身雇用制度が廃れてきたことで、日本の雇用市場はよりダイナミックだが予測しづらいものになってきています。

090

乗換案内
Transit Planner App 乗り換え計画提案アプリ

Norikaeannai is the brand name of a useful transit planning app that can show you how to travel throughout Japan using buses, trains, and even airplanes.

乗換案内は、便利な交通機関利用計画アプリの商品名で、バスや列車、飛行機さえをも乗り継いで日本中を移動する方法を示してくれる。

Thanks to **Transit Planner App**, not only did I not have to worry about getting lost, but I could also figure out exactly which train car to board to get off closest to the elevator.

乗換案内のおかげで、道に迷う心配がないだけでなく、どの車両に乗ればエレベーターに一番近いところで降りられるかまで正確に把握できました。

大名
feudal land-owning magnate 封建時代の大物土地所有者

Daimyō were powerful feudal warlords who ruled over the provinces of Japan from the 10th century through the middle of the 19th century.

大名は、強大な権力を持つ封建武将で、10世紀から19世紀半ばまで日本各地を支配した。

A restored garden in the city center was once part of an estate belonging to a **feudal land-owning magnate**.

市の中心部に復元された庭園は、かつて大名の所有地の一部でした。

浮世
fleeting human journey　はかない人の生涯

Ukiyo, literally translated as "floating world," described the worldly pleasures experienced as part of everyday life during the Edo period. Today, it mainly means a human's earthly life.

浮世は、直訳すると「浮いている世の中」で、江戸時代の日常生活の一部で経験された世俗的な楽しみ方を表していた。今日では、主に人の現世を表す。

Did the participants in **fleeting human journey** culture experience regular joy, or were they simply drowning in the despair of ennui?

浮世文化に身をゆだねた人たちは、常に喜びを感じていたのでしょうか、それとも単に退屈の絶望感の中で身動きが取れなかったのでしょうか。

和
peaceful, harmonious conformity
平和で調和の取れた順応

Wa is harmony within social groups, and it is an integral characteristic of Japanese society.

和とは社会集団の中での調和のことで、日本社会に不可欠な特徴である。

As an American, individualism is considered an advantage, so when I was hired at a company in Japan fresh out of college, it was a struggle to embrace **peaceful, harmonious conformity** like my Japanese coworkers.

アメリカ人にとっては、個人主義が有利だと考えられています。だから、大学を出たてで日本の会社に採用された当時、私には日本人の同僚たちのように和を重んじるのが大変でした。

Chapter
6

Person/People
人

イケメン

091

cool, handsome heartthrob

かっこよくハンサムな憧れの的

 文で説明してみよう！

Ikemen, a portmanteau of "iketeru," "men," and also "men (face)," describes good-looking, sharply dressed, manly men.

イケメンは、「イケてる」とmen、さらには「面」の合成語で、面貌に優れ、格好良く装った、男らしい男を表す。

 ３語フレーズを会話で使おう！

Sachiko's professor was such a **cool, handsome heartthrob** that whenever he called on her, her tongue became completely tied.

サチコの担当教授はあまりにもイケメンだったので、呼びかけられるたびに、彼女はしどろもどろになってしまいました。

Andrew's Point

You can thank my wife for stepping in and rejecting my initial three-word expression: "100% Andrew Robbins." (I reluctantly agree.) There is no true equivalent of *ikemen* in English for a number of reasons. *Ikemen* often implies a combination of good looks, charm, and a kind of elegant or refined masculinity, not captured by words like "hunk" or "stud." Indeed, these terms bring to mind a more muscular or rugged appearance. *Ikemen* incorporates fashion sense and sometimes even someone's voice. In other words, *ikemen* seems to be "the full package" rather than just an attractive male attribute or two.

私が最初に思いついたこの言葉の3語フレーズの候補に、妻が横からダメ出ししたことに感謝してください。何しろ**100% Andrew Robbins**というフレーズだったので（私も不本意ながらダメ出しに従います）。イケメンはしばしば、見た目の良さ、魅力、そしてエレガントで洗練された男らしさが交ざっていることをにおわせます。**hunk**や**stud**といった単語では言い表せないニュアンスです。実際、これらの単語はより筋肉隆々で無骨な外見を思い起こさせるのですから。イケメンという語は、ファッションセンスや時には声が良いという意味合いまで含みます。言い換えれば、イケメンは魅力的な男性が単に1つか2つの特徴を備えているということではなく、「あらゆる特徴を完全に備えている」ことを意味するのです。

イクメン

actively involved father

積極的に父親として関与する人

文で説明してみよう！

Ikumen, a portmanteau of "ikuji" and "men" as well as a play on the word "ikemen," describes men who are actively involved in raising their children and taking care of household chores.

イクメンとは、「育児」とmenの合成語であると同時に「イケメン」をもじったものでもあり、育児や家事に積極的に関与する男性を指す。

3語フレーズを会話で使おう！

Her husband long since fast asleep, Hiroko sighed with her hands deep in dirty dishes, wishing for a time when **actively involved fathers** were the norm rather than the exception.

夫はとっくに眠り込んでおり、ヒロコは汚れた食器に手を突っ込みながらため息をついて、イクメンが特別ではなく当たり前の時代が来ることを願いました。

Andrew's Point

Out of all of the terms in this book, this is the one I like the least. Let me explain. I completely agree that an actively involved father is a good thing. I do most of the cooking in my house, give my kids a bath, do a lot of the cleaning and the laundry—sometimes, it doesn't leave a lot of time for work (much to the chagrin of my editor and publisher). So, the problem I have is that this word has to exist. In other words, there are so few actively involved fathers that we must highlight those who are doing things well. I get it, though. Society takes time to change, and to realize that change, it needs to be pushed in a variety of ways. Therefore, I believe that this word has an overall positive impact. But that it exists is a reminder of the inequality that persists.

本書で取り上げた言葉の中で、私が一番気に入らないのがこれです。説明しましょう。積極的に父親として家庭に関与することが良い、ということには、まったく同意します。うちでは、私がほとんどの料理をこなし、子供たちを風呂に入れ、掃除と洗濯をします——ときどき、そのせいであまり仕事に時間を割けませんが。そこで私が感じる問題点は、このような言葉が存在しなければならないということです。つまり、積極的に父親として家庭に関与している人があまりにも少ないので、うまくやっている父親を強調しなければならないわけです。まあ、それも分かります。社会が変わるには時間がかかるし、その変化を起こすには、いろいろなやり方で後押しする必要があります。だから、この言葉は全体的に前向きな影響を与えていると信じています。とはいえ、この言葉の存在によって、依然として不平等があることを思い出すのです。

おたく

awkward single-subject maniac
やっかいなワンテーマ愛好家

 文で説明してみよう！

Otaku are people who are obsessed with particular interests, from anime and manga to railways to idols.

おたくとは、アニメや漫画、鉄道からアイドルまで、特定の興味の対象に取りつかれている人たちのこと。

 3語フレーズを会話で使おう！

When the local limited express train made its final stop ever at the terminal, the platform was jam-packed with **awkward single-subject maniacs** snapping pictures of the event.

地元の特急列車が終着駅に最後の到着を果たしたとき、プラットホームはこの瞬間を写真を収めようとするおたくたちでごった返しました。

Andrew's Point

I feel conflicted about this expression because of changing perceptions of *otaku*. Outside of Japan in particular, where "otaku" has become a loan word, people often use "otaku" as a badge of pride. And even inside Japan, I don't believe "awkward" applies to all *otaku*. There are some famous *otaku*, like *Shokotan*, that seem perfectly socially capable. By the way, I was plenty awkward as a kid—and possibly now as well—and very likely would have become a video game *otaku*. I played *Final Fantasy* and *Dragon Quest* as much as I possibly could. But when my parents grew concerned that I might be spending too much time playing games, they took my NES and SNES away. Maybe it was for the best. But I still love both series.

私がこの表現に迷いを覚えるのは、おたくの認識が変化しているからです。特に「おたく」という言葉が外来語として定着してきた諸外国では、「おたく」が勲章のように使われることが多いのです。また、日本国内でも、すべてのおたくにawkward（やっかいな、扱いにくい）が当てはまるとは思いません。しょこたんのような有名なおたくもいて、すっかり社会に受け入れられています。ちなみに、私は子供の頃——おそらく今も——かなりawkwardで、ビデオゲームおたくになっていてもおかしくないほどでした。「ファイナルファンタジー」や「ドラゴンクエスト」を、できるときにはいつでもやっていました。でも、私がゲームに時間を費やしすぎているのではないかと心配した両親は、私からファミコンやスーパーファミコンを取り上げてしまいました。たぶん、それが最善策だったのでしょう。でも、私は今でも両シリーズとも大好きです。

オヤジ

094

uncool middle-aged man
やぼったい中年男

文で説明してみよう！

Oyaji is a blanket and often derogatory term for middle-aged men, old men, fathers, bosses, and even proprietors.

オヤジは、中年男性、老人、父親、上司、さらには店主を指す、包括的で時に侮蔑的な言葉である。

３語フレーズを会話で使おう！

I was shocked and disheartened when I was walking my dog and a kid on a bike yelled, "Hey you **uncool middle-aged man**! Get out of my way!"

犬の散歩をしていたら、自転車に乗った子供に「おい、オヤジ！邪魔だよ！」と怒鳴りつけられ、ショックを受けて意気消沈してしまいました。

Andrew's Point

This is a rare case where I felt that three words were too many to accurately describe the term. What's important aside from the age, gender, potential relationship, and, perhaps, lack of coolness is that, in some cases, *oyaji* is used affectionately. There's a single word in British English that seems to capture all of this: geezer. ("Old man," though two words, also seems to do the trick in British.) Geezer in American English isn't used affectionately, and it generally refers to a man who is odd, eccentric, or unreasonable. It's often used derogatorily as "old geezer."

これは、元の日本語を正確に表現するのに3つの言葉では多すぎると感じた珍しい例です。年齢、性別、話者との関係、そしておそらくは格好良さの欠如、といった点はさておき、重要なのは、おやじが愛情を込めて使われる場合があるということです。イギリス英語に、これらすべての要素を包含する単語があります。**geezer** がそれです（old man という2語のフレーズにも、イギリス英語では同じニュアンスがあるようです）。しかし、米語では **geezer** が愛情を込めて使われることはなく、一般的には風変わりな人、変人、あるいは理不尽な人を指します。よく **old geezer** の形で侮蔑的に使われます。

フリーター

semi-permanent part-time worker

半永久的なアルバイト従業員

文で説明してみよう！

Furītā are those who choose to work part-time jobs, whether they are putting off starting a career, trying to pursue loftier goals like becoming a writer or a musician, or are lacking the skills or opportunities to find more consistent work.

フリーターとは、アルバイトで働くことを選択する人たちのことで、就職を先延ばしにしている人もいれば、作家やミュージシャンのようなさらなる高みを目指している人もいれば、より安定した職に就けるだけの技能や機会に恵まれない人もいる。

3語フレーズを会話で使おう！

The rise of the gig economy has played a significant role in supporting a new generation of **semi-permanent part-time workers**.

ギグエコノミーの台頭は、新世代のフリーターを支える上で重要な役割を果たしています。

Andrew's Point

The scope of *furītā* is broad, including unemployed, underemployed, and not fully-employed people. The term's connotations have also changed over time. During the bubble economy, it was positively associated with people exploring unconventional employment options, often for fun. Afterward, it was negatively associated with people perceived as burdens on society. Three words can't capture all of this. I was tempted to write something like "life ain't work," but that's more of a commentary on *furītā* philosophy than an explanation of *furītā* themselves. In the end, I felt "semi-permanent part-time workers" covered the most ground.

フリーターの範囲は広く、失業者、非正規従業員、非常勤従業員を含みます。この言葉の意味合いも時代とともに変化してきました。バブル期には、旧来のものとは異なる雇用形態を時に遊び感覚で模索する人たちを、肯定的なニュアンスで連想させる言葉でした。その後、社会のお荷物と見なされる人々と否定的に結び付けられました。3語でこうしたことのすべてを表現することはできません。私は「人生は仕事じゃない」といったことが伝わる表現を出そうと試みたのですが、それではフリーター自体の説明ではなく、フリーターの哲学へのコメントになってしまいます。結局、**semi-permanent part-time worker** が一番的を射ていると感じました。

ペーパードライバー

096

zero-experience licensed driver
無経験の運転免許保持者

 文で説明してみよう！

Pēpādoraibā are people who are licensed drivers by definition only as they have little to no experience actually driving.

ペーパードライバーとは、実際に車を運転した経験がほとんどないのに、名目上だけ運転免許を持っている人のこと。

 ３語フレーズを会話で使おう！

It's absurd that my best friend, a **zero-experience licensed driver** who has never even owned a car, acquired a Japanese gold license, even though I've driven hundreds of thousands of miles and only got into one minor fender bender.

ばかばかしいことに、私の親友はペーパードライバーで車を持ったことすらないのに、日本のゴールド免許を持っており、一方で私は、何十万キロもの運転経験があり、たった一度軽い接触事故を起こしただけなのにゴールド免許保持者ではないのです。

Andrew's Point

Although you might expect every adult in the U.S. to drive, that's not actually the case. There are plenty of people who live in big cities, like New York City, who get by just fine with walking and public transportation. Some of them do have licenses, however, as it's useful to have as a form of ID. I had a driver's license when I lived in Japan, but I never made use of it. I didn't even have to take a driver's license test because my home state of Maryland has a reciprocity agreement with Japan. I haven't driven a car in several years. Does that make me a "born-again zero-experience licensed driver"?

アメリカではすべての成人が車を運転すると思うかもしれませんが、実はそんなことはありません。ニューヨークのような大都市に住んでいて、徒歩や公共交通機関の利用だけで十分やっていける人がたくさんいるのです。しかし、そういう人たちの中にも免許証保持者はいます。身分証明書として持っていると便利だからです。私は日本に住んでいたとき、運転免許証を持っていましたが、一度も使いませんでした。故郷のメリーランド州が日本と互恵協約を結んでいるので、運転免許の試験を受ける必要さえありませんでした。だから、もう何年も車を運転していません。これでは私は「生まれ変わったペーパードライバー」でしょうか。

ママ友

097

mama group member
母親グループのメンバー

文で説明してみよう！

Mamatomo, a portmanteau of "mama" and "tomodachi," are the mothers that bond through shared parenting experiences, playdates, and mutual support in their children's upbringing.

ママ友は、mama と「友だち」の合成語で、子育ての経験を共有したり、交流したり、支え合ったりすることを通じて結束する母親たちである。

3語フレーズを会話で使おう！

When I went to pick my son up from kindergarten, I felt somewhat out of place amidst the pockets of chatting **mama group members**.

息子を幼稚園に迎えに行くと、おしゃべりをするママ友たちの間でどうにも場違いな思いを抱きました。

Andrew's Point

Whenever I went to my sons' Japanese kindergarten to pick them up after school, I always marveled at the pockets of *mamatomo* buzzing with conversation about the latest trend or rumor or what have you. Occasionally, I would greet one or two or exchange some useful tidbit I came across, but I somehow felt unwelcome in their collective huddle. Perhaps I felt intimidated. I wonder why there were no *papatomo* groups. All of the papas seemed content to stand around looking at their smartphones (myself included). The grandmas didn't try to infiltrate the ranks of *mamatomo* either. They seemed content to enjoy the brief serenity before the school door opened and unleashed a screaming hoard of young agents of chaos.

息子たちが通う日本の幼稚園に放課後、彼らを迎えに行くと、ママ友の集団が最新のトレンドや人のうわさなどの話題で盛り上がっているのに驚かされました。まれに、1人か2人とあいさつを交わしたり、ちょっとした役立つ情報を交換したりすることもありましたが、私は何となく、彼女らの集団に歓迎されていないように感じました。たぶん私はおじけづいていたのです。なぜパパ友の集団がなかったのでしょうか。パパたちは皆、甘んじて遠巻きに立ち、スマホを眺めているようでした（私も含めて）。おばあちゃんたちもママ友の仲間には入ろうとせず、幼稚園のドアが開いて絶叫する幼いカオスの代理人たちの大群が解放されるまでの束の間の平穏を、楽しんでいるように見えました。

ヤンキー

098

Japanese juvenile delinquent

日本の不良少年少女

文で説明してみよう！

A *yankī* is a juvenile delinquent, one who is often dressed in flashy clothing.

ヤンキーとは不良少年少女のことで、ど派手な服装をしていることが多い。

３語フレーズを会話で使おう！

What impresses me most about the **Japanese juvenile delinquents** is their ability to look cool while squatting.

ヤンキーについて一番感心するのは、しゃがんでいても格好良く見せられる点です。

Andrew's Point

I decided not to avoid using the word "Japanese" for this term because I feel that *yankī* have a distinctive style that should be differentiated from track-suit-wearing Russian juvenile delinquents and soccer-jersey-wearing British juvenile delinquents. Maybe it's due to *anime*, *manga*, and media, but *yankī* seem to have a sort of unique charm or a sense of nostalgic allure despite their notorious reputation. I wonder if adults of all cultures secretly envy the rebelliousness of such loutish youth. By the way, had I not decided to include "Japanese," I would have used "loutish."

この言葉については **Japanese** という語を外さないことに決めました。というのも、ヤンキーには、トレーニングウエアの上下を着たロシアの不良少年少女や、サッカーのユニフォームを着たイギリスの不良少年少女とは一線を画すべき、独特のスタイルがあるように感じるからです。アニメや漫画、メディアの影響もあるのかもしれませんが、ヤンキーには、その悪評に反して、ある種の独特の魅力というか郷愁を誘う魅惑的なものがあるように思います。どんな文化圏の大人も、そんな無作法な若者たちの反骨精神を密かにうらやんでいるのではないでしょうか。ちなみに、**Japanese** を用いないとすれば、**loutish**（無作法な）を使っていたでしょう。

帰国子女

099

repatriated young national

海外から帰還した若い自国民

 文で説明してみよう！

Kikokushijo are children of Japanese expatriates who have been educated outside of Japan and then repatriated.

帰国子女とは、海外に居住していた日本人の子弟で、日本国外で教育を受けた後、帰国した人のことである。

 ３語フレーズを会話で使おう！

Repatriated young nationals grow to become invaluable assets to corporate Japan with their keen understanding of cultures at home and abroad.

帰国子女は、国内外の文化に精通していることで、単一指向性の日本にとってかけがえのない財産になるべく育つのです。

Andrew's Point

My initial expression was "repatriated Japanese children." Then, I realized that the general concept is not unique to Japan. Regardless, I find *kikokushijo* truly fascinating. When I taught at a small *eikaiwa* school in the mid-2000s, a young woman had just returned from the U.S. and joined one of my classes. Her American accent was flawless. I often told jokes in her class and expected her to get them, but those jokes frequently fell flat. At first, I thought my jokes were just bad, but then I realized that she didn't understand my American sarcasm either. I had judged her to understand American culture based on her flawless accent alone, and I had been mistaken (Also, my jokes were probably bad).

私が当初考えた表現は、**repatriated Japanese children** でした。その後、この概念の大枠は日本独自のものではないと気づきました。ともあれ、私には帰国子女が実に魅力的に見えます。2000年代半ばに小さな英会話学校で教えていたころ、アメリカから帰国したばかりの若い女性が私のクラスの一つに入ってきました。彼女のアメリカ英語は完璧でした。私は彼女のいるクラスでよくジョークを飛ばし、それらが彼女に通じることを期待したのですが、ジョークは往々にして彼女にはウケませんでした。最初、私のジョークが単に面白くないだけだと思ったのですが、そのうちに彼女が私のアメリカ流の皮肉を理解していないという面もあることに気づきました。私は彼女が話す非の打ちどころのないアメリカ英語を根拠に、アメリカ文化が分かるはずだと思い込んでいたのですが、それは間違いだったのです（たぶん私のジョークも悪かったのでしょうが）。

巫女

100

Shintō shrine priestess

神社の女性神宮

文で説明してみよう！

A *miko* is a young priestess who works at a Shintō shrine, generally tasked with trivial or mundane duties.

巫女とは、神社で働く若い女性聖職者のことで、一般的には些事や雑用を担う。

3語フレーズを会話で使おう！

When I learned that some **Shintō shrine priestesses** are essentially students working a part-time job like any other, it stripped them of some of their mystique.

巫女の一部は、本当の身分が学生で、他の学生と同様にアルバイトをしているのだと知ったとき、巫女の神秘性がいくぶん失われてしまいました。

Andrew's Point

"Were this the twentieth century, I likely would have gone with "Shintō shrine maiden." Many texts have used that language—and some even continue to do so to this day. You can Google it for yourself. The problem is that the term "maiden" might be seen today as perpetuating a limited and traditional view of women's roles. It diminishes the significance of a *miko*'s duties and responsibilities and instead emphasizes youth and marital status. Yes, it may be true that *miko* are young and unmarried, but that's not all that they are. The term "priestess" better acknowledges their training, skills, and contributions to Shintō rituals and ceremonies.

今が20世紀だったら、**Shintō shrine maiden** としたでしょう。多くの文章でこの表現が使われてきました──それに、現在でも依然としてそう表現している資料があります。**Google** で検索してみてください。問題は、**maiden**（未婚女性）という言葉によって、いまだに女性の役割に関する限定的かつ古臭い見方が変わっていないように見られてしまうかもしれないということです。そのことで、巫女の任務や責任の重要性が薄らぎ、代わりに若さや婚姻状況が強調されてしまいます。ええ、確かに巫女は若くて未婚ですが、それが巫女の全てではありません。**priestess** という言葉のほうが、巫女の修行や技能、神道の儀式や式典への貢献をより正当に評価するものです。

101

AKB48
Female Idol Group 女性アイドルグループ

📄 *AKB48* is a group of young female entertainers who sing and dance to Japanese pop music.

AKB48は、若い女性エンターテイナーのグループで、日本語のポップミュージックを歌い、それに合わせて踊る。

💬 Though all members of the **Female Idol Group** are attractive, it has been said that the organization avoids recruiting women who could be considered too beautiful lest they take on an aura of unattainability.

AKB48の全メンバーが魅力的ですが、マネジメントサイドは美人すぎる女性の採用を避けていると言われています。グループが、手の届かない存在であるかのような雰囲気を醸さないようにしているのです。

ダウンタウン
Iconic Comedy Duo 象徴的な2人組コメディアン

📄 *Dauntaun* is one of Japan's most prolific and influential comedy duos.

ダウンタウンは、日本で最も売れていて影響力のある2人組コメディアンの一組である。

💬 Subtitled videos of **Iconic Comedy Duo** on YouTube appeal to a wide audience overseas.

字幕付きでYouTubeにアップされているダウンタウンの動画は、海外の幅広い視聴者にウケています。

お笑い芸人
variety show comedian バラエティー番組のコメディアン

📄 *Owarai geinin* are comedians who, in addition to their acts, often appear on TV variety programs to add some spice to the conversation.

お笑い芸人とはコメディアンのことで、芸のかたわらテレビのバラエティ
番組によく出演し、話の盛り上げ役になる。

I remember laughing so hard when I first saw that one **variety show
comedian**, but one year later, I found him to be dull and uninspired.

あるお笑い芸人を初めて見たとき大笑いしたのを覚えていますが、1年後には、そ
の人は退屈でぱっとしないと感じました。

先輩・後輩
senior and junior 年長者と年少者

The hierarchical relationship of *senpai kōhai* exists in
almost every type of Japanese organization, from school
and sports to business and politics.

先輩・後輩という上下関係は、学校からスポーツ界、政財界に至るまで、
あらゆる種類の日本の組織に存在する。

The bond between the **senior and junior** members of the team as
well as their range of perspectives contributed significantly to their
overall success on the project.

チームの先輩・後輩のきずなが、彼らの視野の広さと相まって、プロジェクトの
全体的な成功に大きく貢献しました。

白バイ
white police motorcycle 白い警察用オートバイ

Shirobai, a portmanteau of "shiro" and "bike", are large,
white, easily-identifiable motorcycles ridden by police
officers.

白バイは、「白」とbikeの合成語で、警察官が乗る、大型で白く、すぐにそ
れと分かるオートバイである。

Compared to **white police motorcycles**, which convey a
commanding sense of authority, diminutive police scooters bring
to mind fast food delivery.

権威を感じさせる白バイに比べると、小型の警察用スクーターはファーストフー
ドのデリバリーを連想させます。

102

八重歯
crooked tooth beauty　曲がった歯の美

Yaeba refers to teeth—typically canines—that protrude, often due to being pushed forward by other teeth because of a lack of space.

八重歯とは、歯——一般的に犬歯——が突き出した状態を指す。口腔内が狭いために他の歯に押されて飛び出すことが多い。

Crooked tooth beauty may be considered cute in Japan, but in countries where dental hygiene and tooth alignment are associated with socioeconomic status, it is not attractive.

八重歯は、日本ではかわいいと見なされるかもしれませんが、歯の衛生状態や歯並びが社会経済的地位と関連している国々では、魅力的ではないのです。

宝塚歌劇団
All-Female Theatre Troupe　女性のみの演劇一座

Founded in 1913, the *Takarazuka Kagekidan* is an all-female musical theatre troupe based in the city of Takarazuka in Hyōgo Prefecture.

1913年に創立された宝塚歌劇団は、兵庫県宝塚市を本拠地とする女性だけの音楽劇団である。

As a man, it hurts my pride to see the women of the **All-Female Theatre Troupe** portraying men cooler than I could ever hope to be.

男として、宝塚歌劇団の女性たちが、自分がこうありたいと望む姿よりも格好良い男性を演じているのを見ると、プライドが傷ついてしまいます。

坊っちゃん
Japanese Holden Caulfield　日本のホールデン・コールフィールド

Bocchan is the protagonist of the eponymous novel by famed Japanese author Natsume Sōseki.

坊っちゃんは、著名な日本人作家、夏目漱石の同名小説の主人公である。

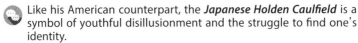 Like his American counterpart, the *Japanese Holden Caulfield* is a symbol of youthful disillusionment and the struggle to find one's identity.

坊っちゃんは、アメリカのホールデン・コールフィールドと同様に、若者の幻滅と、自分らしさを見いだそうとする葛藤の象徴です。

アイヌ
Indigenous Northern People 先住北方民

The *Ainu* are indigenous people of northern Japan with a culture distinct from that of other Japanese.

アイヌは、他の日本人とは異なる文化を持つ北日本の先住民族である。

These days, some people are working hard to preserve the language and culture of the **Indigenous Northern People**.

近年、アイヌの言葉や文化を守ろうと賢明に努力している人たちがいます。

腐女子
female yaoi consumer 女性のやおい消費者

Fujoshi refers to women often in their late teens and 20s who are fans of media that revolve around romantic relationships between men.

腐女子は、10代後半から20代に多い、男性同士の恋愛関係を扱ったメディアのファンの女性を指す。

As boys love *manga* has gained a significant chunk of the market, the stigma around **female yaoi consumers** has started to erode.

ボーイズラブの漫画が市場で大きなシェアを占めるようになり、腐女子にまつわる悪いイメージが払拭され始めています。

103

サラリーマン
loyal corporate worker 忠誠心のある企業従業員

Sararīman describes a loyal corporate worker who typically puts in egregiously long hours, valuing work and loyalty to the company above all else.

サラリーマンとは、忠誠心の強い企業従業員で、たいてい長時間労働に従事し、仕事と会社への忠誠心を何よりも重視する。

After I quit the conservative company to which I devoted two decades of my life, I started my own company, and though I put in even longer hours, I still felt liberated, having shed the skin of an everyday **loyal corporate worker**.

人生のうちの20年間を捧げた保守的な会社を辞め、自分の会社を立ち上げると、労働時間はさらに長くなりましたが、それでも平凡なサラリーマンから脱皮した解放感に浸りました。

Chapter
7

Place/Location
場所・施設

カプセルホテル

104

coffin-sized sleeping accommodation

ひつぎサイズの睡眠用宿泊施設

 文で説明してみよう！

Kapuseru hoteru are a budget-friendly type of accommodation that offer guests basic amenities and single-person beds in tiny private capsules.

カプセルホテルは、財布に優しい宿泊施設の一種で、基本的なアメニティーと1人用のベッドを備えた超小型の個人用カプセルである。

 3語フレーズを会話で使おう！

Coffin-sized sleeping accommodations are equally a budget hunter's dream and a claustrophobe's nightmare.

カプセルホテルは、安さを追求する人にとっての夢であると同時に、閉所恐怖症の人にとっての悪夢でもあります。

Andrew's Point

I have a confession: despite having lived in Japan for 17 years, I have not once visited a *kapuseru hoteru*. It's not that I'm claustrophobic or anything—far from it. I actually like the idea of a cozy, coffin-like space (well, maybe not as small as a real coffin). In fact, one of the most satisfying slumbers I ever had was in a tiny closet in my college dormitory (alcohol may have been involved). Anyway, my issue is that staying at a *kapuseru hoteru* is a gamble. You won't know until it's too late whether you have a heavy snorer on one side or perhaps a sleep talker on the other. I value sleep too much to take that risk.

私は日本に17年間住んだにもかかわらず、一度もカプセルホテルを利用したことがありません。閉所恐怖症だとかそういうことは、まったくありません。むしろ私は居心地の良い、ひつぎのような空間(まあ、たぶん本物のひつぎほどは狭くないでしょうが)という発想が好きです。事実、私がこれまでに経験した中で最も満足した眠りは、大学の寮のちっぽけなクローゼットの中でのものでした(飲酒の影響もあったかもしれませんが)。とにかく、私が言いたいのは、カプセルホテルに泊まるのは賭けだということです。隣にいびきのひどい人がいるか、あるいは反対側の隣に寝言を言う人がいるか、分かったときにはもう手遅れなのですから。私にとって睡眠は非常に重要なので、そんなリスクは冒せないのです。

ソープランド

body-cleansing prostitution establishment
体を洗う売春施設

 文で説明してみよう！

Sōpurando describes a brothel that adopts the guise of a full-service bathing facility to circumvent laws outlawing prostitution.

ソープランドとは、売春を違法化する法律を回避するために、フルサービスの入浴施設を装った売春宿のことで、売春を禁じる法律の裏をかいたものである。

 ３語フレーズを会話で使おう！

Some people may visit **body-cleansing prostitution establishments** for sexual gratification, but Jeff just likes a thorough, head-to-toe cleaning performed by a professional.

性欲を満たすためにソープランドを訪れる人もいるかもしれませんが、ジェフは単に、プロの手で頭のてっぺんからつま先まで徹底的に洗ってもらうことが好きなのです。

Andrew's Point

I'm slightly dissatisfied with what I came up with here because it leaves out an important—and fascinating—aspect of *sōpurand*. They are legal loopholes. (I also would have liked to include "loopholes" because it includes the word "holes," but that's beside the point.) *Sōpurando* exist as establishments to provide a façade service—body-cleansing—for a fee while actually treading through a legal gray area to provide access to prostitution. So, I apologize for describing something so spicy with words that sound so mundane.

ここに出したフレーズには少々不満です。なぜなら、ソープランドに関するある重要な——しかも魅力的な——側面を省いてしまっているからです。それは loopholes（法の抜け穴）です（loopholes には holes という言葉が含まれているということも、この語を省きたくなかった理由ですが、それはさておき）。ソープランドは、表向きは体を洗うサービスを有料で提供する店として存在していますが、一方で実際には、法的なグレーゾーンを超えて売春が行われます。というわけで、非常にきわどい事柄をあまりにも凡庸な言葉で表現することにおわびします。

ハチ公前交差点

106

Tokyo's busiest crossing

東京で一番混雑する横断歩道

 文で説明してみよう！

Located in Tokyo, *hachikōmae kōsaten* is the world's busiest pedestrian crossing, with more than 3,000 people crossing at a time at peak hours.

東京にあるハチ公前交差点は、世界一混雑する横断歩道で、ピーク時には一度に3,000人を超える人が横断する。

 3語フレーズを会話で使おう！

The absurd chaotic fluidity of **Tokyo's busiest crossing** is poetry in motion.

ハチ公前交差点の常軌を逸した無秩序な滑らかさは、動く韻文とでも言うべきものです。

Andrew's Point

My second runner-up was "Tokyo's Times Square" because if we focus solely on the crossing, we lose sight of the urban setting around the crossing. And that setting is iconic, just like its New York counterpart. My third runner-up was "fluid scramble crossing," which focuses on both the chaos and the absurd dance of fluid dynamics personified. But "Tokyo's busiest crossing" was my favorite. Perhaps it lacks grace, but it gets the point across, just as everyone at the crossing gets across to their intended points as well.

私が2つ目の候補として挙げたフレーズは**Tokyo's Times Square**でした。というのも、横断歩道だけに着目すると、その周辺の都市環境に目が向かなくなってしまうからです。しかも、その環境はまさにニューヨークの当該地区と似ているのです。3つ目の候補は**fluid scramble crossing**（流体スクランブル交差点）で、流体力学を擬人化したようなカオスと常軌を逸したダンス様の動きの両方に焦点を当てています。しかし、**Tokyo's busiest crossing**が一番気に入っています。たぶん優美さには欠けますが、ポイントを押さえて（get across）おり、それはまさに交差点にいる誰もがそれぞれ思いどおりの場所へ横断する（get across）のと同様なのです。

銀座

107

Tokyo's Fifth Avenue
東京の 5 番街

 文で説明してみよう！

Built on the site of an Edo-era mint, *Ginza* today is an upscale shopping, dining, and entertainment district in Tokyo.

江戸時代の貨幣鋳造所の跡地が開発されてできた銀座は、現在では東京の高級ショッピング街であり、また飲食街、娯楽街である。

 3 語フレーズを会話で使おう！

As Kazuya glanced at the prices listed on the menu at the upscale restaurant they were at near **Tokyo's Fifth Avenue**, he was grateful that his client was picking up the tab.

カズヤは、銀座近くの高級レストランでメニューに並んだ価格を一瞥しながら、彼の顧客が勘定を持ってくれることに感謝しました。

Andrew's Point

Rather than simply calling this "Tokyo's luxury row," I decided to make a direct comparison to "Fifth Avenue" because it's another iconic shopping district associated with luxury and prestige. They're also both cultural hubs with theaters, art galleries, and cultural events. But, of course, there are clear differences. Fifth Avenue represents the hustle and modernity of New York City with its skyscrapers and American architectural designs, whereas Ginza reflects a blend of traditional and contemporary Japanese aesthetics and sensibilities. As with Fifth Avenue, to understand the vibe, you have to visit.

単純に **Tokyo's luxury row**（東京のぜいたくな街）と呼ぶのではなく、ニューヨークの5番街に直接例えることにしました。なぜなら、5番街もまた、高級感と威信を伴う象徴的なショッピング街だからです。どちらの街もまた、劇場や画廊、文化的なイベントが開催される文化の中心地です。しかし、もちろん明確な違いもあります。5番街では超高層ビルとアメリカ流建築デザインによってニューヨーク市の喧騒と現代性が表れているのに対し、銀座には日本の伝統的な美意識や感性と現代的なそれらの融合が反映されているのです。5番街と同様、その雰囲気を理解するには実際に訪れてみるしかありません。

道頓堀

108

Osaka Food-and-Entertainment Mecca
大阪の食と娯楽の中心地

 文で説明してみよう！

Dōtonbori is a bustling and vibrant Osaka tourist destination chock full of shops, restaurants, and bars.

道頓堀はにぎやかで活気のある大阪の観光地で、店舗やレストラン、酒場がたくさんある。

 ３語フレーズを会話で使おう！

In my early thirties, all too often, I found myself passing through **Osaka Food-and-Entertainment Mecca** in the light of the morning sun as I trudged toward the train home.

30代前半の頃には、何度となく、朝日に照らされた道頓堀を抜け、重い足取りで電車に乗り込み帰宅したものです。

Andrew's Point

I had a lot more energy in my late twenties and early thirties. I also had a lot fewer kids and wives (0 and 0). So, being a denizen of Kansai, I spent a lot of nights in and around Dōtonbori. I saw the sunrise on a few occasions there as well—sometimes from a hotel room, sometimes outside a club, sometimes … sometimes it was just a blur. I never did jump into the river, though. But of course, the Tigers won the Japan Championship series the year before I arrived in Japan and then, again, in 2023, a month after I left. I'm not sure if that means my timing was terrible or great.

私は、20代後半から30代前半にかけては、もっと元気でした。それに、妻子もいませんでした。だから、関西に暮らす身だった私は、道頓堀やその周辺で何夜も過ごしたのです。時には日の出を拝むこともありました——あるときはホテルの部屋から、あるときはクラブの外で、またあるときは……おぼろげな記憶しかありません。川に飛び込むことはありませんでしたが。でももちろん、タイガースは私が来日する前年に日本シリーズで優勝し、2023年にもまた、私が日本を発った1カ月後に勝ちました。つまるところ、私はタイミングが悪かったのか良かったのか、はっきりしませんが。

アメ横
Ameyoko Shopping Street　アメ横買い物街

109

Ameyayokochō, often abbreviated to *Ameyoko*, is a colorful, open-air market located near Ueno Station, full of discounted products, including fashion items, cosmetics, medicines, and even fresh food.

アメ横と略されることが多いアメヤ横丁は、上野駅近くにあるにぎやかな青空市場で、ファッションアイテムから化粧品、医薬品、生鮮食料品に至るまで、値引きされた商品であふれている。

A quick jaunt through **Ameyoko Shopping Street** and Katherine was set with enough makeup for the year.

アメ横をざっと一回りして、キャサリンは1年分の化粧品を買いそろえました。

エステ
beauty enhancement salon　美しさ増進サロン

Esute, short for "aesthetic salons," are popular establishments where people go for mostly non-surgical cosmetic treatments, including facial care and hair removal.

エステとは、aesthetic salons を縮めた言葉で、美顔や脱毛など、主に非外科的な美容処置のために訪れる施設である。

Momoko ducked out to a **beauty enhancement salon** during her lunch break, and when she returned to the office, her eyelashes seemed to have grown to a length both biologically and physically impossible.

モモコは昼休みにエステに出かけたのですが、職場に戻ってくると、まつげが生物学的にも物理的にも不可能な長さまで伸びていました。

キャバクラ
sexy paid flirting セクシーな有料いちゃつき場

Kyabakura, a portmanteau of "cabaret" and "club," is a nightclub where customers—mostly men—pay to drink with and be entertained by attractive hostesses.

キャバクラとは、cabaret と club を合わせた造語で、客――主に男性――がお金を払って魅力的なホステスと飲み、彼女らのもてなしを受けるナイトクラブである。

The man rejected his friends' invitation to **sexy paid flirting**: he preferred chatting up women in bars and cafés where interest in his charms was not feigned for profit.

その男性は、友人たちからキャバクラへ行こうと誘われたものの、断りました。彼はバーやカフェで女性とおしゃべりするほうが好きでした。もうけのために見せかけで自分の魅力に興味を示されたりしない場所だからです。

パワースポット
spiritual energy location 霊的エネルギーの場所

Pawāsupotto are places where one can feel and even absorb some of the concentrated spiritual energy.

パワースポットとは、凝縮された霊的なエネルギーを感じたり、さらには吸収したりできる場所のこと。

Munching on a rice ball on a bench, Joyce felt somehow sacrilegious when a tour group crowded around extolling the virtues of the **spiritual energy location** situated right where she was seated.

ベンチでおにぎりを頬張っていたジョイスは、何となく罰当たりな気分になりました。自分が座っている場所にあるパワースポットの効力を絶賛するツアー客に囲まれたからです。

メイド喫茶
maid waitress café メイドウエートレスカフェ

110

Meidokissa are cafés where women dressed up in maid costumes serve customers.

メイド喫茶とは、メイド服を着た女性が接客するカフェのこと。

Visiting a **maid waitress café** is considered essential to many a foreign *otaku* making his or her way through Japan.

メイド喫茶詣では、日本を旅行する多くの外国人おたくにとって欠かせないと考えられています。

ラブホテル
undercover sex lodge 秘密のセックス小屋

Rabuhoteru are short-stay—and frequently themed—accommodations primarily for the purpose of sexual activities.

ラブホテルとは、短時間利用型の――しかも、多くにコンセプトがある――主に性行為を目的とした休憩宿泊施設のことである。

With no vacancies in the entire city and rain pouring down, the desolate traveler had no choice but to duck into an **undercover sex lodge** for the night.

町中どこを探しても宿に空室がなく、雨が降りしきる中、その一人旅行者は、一晩ラブホテルに投宿するしかありませんでした。

漫画喫茶
manga library café 漫画図書館カフェ

Mangakissa, short for "manga kissaten," are establishments where customers can pay by the hour to read from an extensive library of *manga*, watch DVDs, surf the Internet, and, in some cases, even spend the night.

漫画喫茶とは、「漫画喫茶店」を縮めた形で、客が時間単位でお金を払い、豊富な漫画の蔵書を読んだり、DVDを見たり、インターネットを閲覧したり、場合によっては寝泊まりしたりもできる店である。

Mana walked into the sprawling **manga library café** and couldn't contain her bubbling excitement: she had found her Shangri-la.

マナは雑然とした漫画喫茶に足を踏み入れ、湧き上がる興奮を抑えきれませんでした。そこは彼女にとっての理想郷だったのです。

秋葉原電気街
Akihabara Electric Town 秋葉原電気街

Akihabara Denkigai is located in the Akihabara district of Tokyo and is known for its tightly packed buildings full of electronics, games, *anime*, and other eclectic merchandise.

秋葉原電気街は東京の秋葉原地区にあり、電子機器やゲーム機器、アニメ関連品、その他さまざまな電気製品が、狭く立て込んだビルの中で大量に売られていることで知られる。

I found a grail item deep in the recesses of **Akihabara Electric Town**: a Nintendo Playstation prototype that never found its way to the consumer market.

私は、秋葉原電気街の奥深くで、ある聖杯とも言うべき品物を見つけました。任天堂プレイステーションのプロトタイプで、一般消費者市場に出回ることのなかったものです。

111

浅草寺
Tokyo's Oldest Temple 東京最古の寺院

🔖 *Sensōji* is a popular sightseeing spot featuring an iconic red paper lantern and a bustling market.

浅草寺は、特徴的な赤いちょうちんと、にぎやかな仲見世で知られる人気の観光スポットである。

💬 Whenever I visit **Tokyo's Oldest Temple**, I always give a little bow to Fūjin-sama and Raijin-sama, obscured in the shadows of the Kaminarimon gate.

私は浅草寺を訪れるといつも、雷門の影に隠れて見えにくい風神さまと雷神さまに小さくお辞儀をします。

東京スカイツリー
Japan's Tallest Tower 日本一高い塔

🔖 *Tōkyō Sukai Tsurī* is the tallest tower in Japan, measuring 634 meters.

東京スカイツリーは日本で最も高い塔で、高さ634メートルである。

💬 What I love about **Japan's Tallest Tower** is the way its colorful lights interact with the lattice structure and make it come alive at night.

私が東京スカイツリーでとても気に入っているのは、夜になると色とりどりの照明が格子構造と相互に作用し、塔が生き生きと浮かび上がるところです。

東京タワー
Tokyo's Eiffel Tower 東京のエッフェル塔

🔖 Built in 1958, *Tōkyō Tawā* is a communications and observation tower.

1958年に建設された東京タワーは、通信および展望のための塔である。

💬 When I stepped out of the bar for a smoke and mistook **Tokyo's Eiffel Tower** for the Eiffel Tower in Paris, I knew it was time to call it a night.

一服しようとバーから出て、東京タワーをパリのエッフェル塔と見間違えたとき、今日はもう飲むのをやめようと思いました。

銭湯
communal ablution spot　公共の体を洗う場所

Unlike *onsen*, which are natural springs, *sentō* are public bathhouses, originally built to cater to the masses that did not have baths in their own homes.

天然の湧き水を使った温泉とは異なり、銭湯は公衆浴場で、元々は自宅に風呂を持たない大衆のために設けられたものだった。

My friends back in Ireland would never believe it if I told them I'd dip out of work during my lunch break to relax for a spell at a **communal ablution spot**.

私が昼休みに仕事を抜け出して銭湯でしばしくつろいでいると言っても、アイルランドにいる友人たちは信じないでしょう。

温 泉
natural hot spring　天然温泉

Whether indoor or outdoor, *onsen* are hot springs that make use of naturally hot water from geothermally-heated springs.

屋内外を問わず、温泉は地熱で温められた源泉由来の天然の湯を用いた熱い湧き水である。

My second-most memorable **natural hot spring** experience is when I went to Aomori and sunk my body into a bath full of 100-odd apples bobbing in the water.

私の2番目に印象深い温泉体験は、青森に行って100個余りのリンゴが浮かぶ風呂に体を沈めたことです。

露天風呂
open-air hot-spring bath 屋外温泉風呂

112

Rotenburo, literally translated as "open-air baths," are hot-spring baths situated outdoors.

露天風呂とは、直訳すると「屋外の風呂」で、戸外に設けられた温泉浴場である。

There are few pleasures greater than soaking in an **open-air hot-spring bath** amidst gentle falling snow.

深々と降る雪の中で露天風呂に浸かる以上の喜びなど、ほとんどありません。

Chapter
8

Sports/Performing Arts
スポーツ・芸能

駅伝

long-distance relay race
長距離リレー競走

文で説明してみよう！

Ekiden are long-distance relay races often held on roads.

駅伝は長距離のリレー競走で、たいてい一般道で行われる。

３語フレーズを会話で使おう！

Although I don't care much for watching sports on TV, I couldn't help but get caught up in the excitement and the drama while watching the Hakone **long-distance relay race** with my family.

私はあまりテレビでスポーツを見ようと思わないのですが、箱根駅伝を家族と見ていると、その高揚感とドラマ性に魅了されずにはいられませんでした。

Andrew's Point

I love *ekiden*. Many years ago, before I became a runner, I would always get caught up in the drama watching each year's race. When I turned 32, I picked up running to stay in shape and have since run 11 full marathons in Japan. Over time, I learned to understand the agony and the triumph that accompanies a long race. And while I've had the privilege of making running friends, running with them, and supporting them, I've always wanted to experience the camaraderie that comes with an *ekiden*. And it turns out that I can! My cousin Zack recently told me about his experience running in the Hood to Coast, a 198-mile relay that takes place in Oregon, extending from Mt. Hood to the Pacific coast. I can't wait to try it.

私は駅伝が大好きです。ランナーになるずっと前、毎年のレースを見ては、そのドラマ性に夢中になっていました。32歳になって、健康維持のためにランニングを始め、以来、日本で11回フルマラソンを走りました。そのうちに、長いレースに伴う苦しみと勝利の喜びを理解できるようになりました。そして、ランニング仲間を作り、一緒に走り、応援する機会に恵まれる一方で、駅伝のような仲間意識を体験したいとずっと思っていました。そして、それが実現可能であることが分かったのです！　いとこのザックが最近、「フッド・トゥ・コースト」を走った経験について話してくれました。オレゴン州で開催される198マイルのリレーで、フッド山から太平洋岸まで走るものです。私も参加を待ちきれません。

漫才

two-person stand-up comedy
２人スタンドアップコメディー

文で説明してみよう！

Manzai is a type of two-person comedy that features the interactions between a straight role and a funny role.

漫才は２人で演じるコメディーの一種で、まともな役とふざけた役のやりとりが特徴である。

３語フレーズを会話で使おう！

Compared to American stand-up, the **two-person stand-up comedy** of Japan tends to explore less provocative content in favor of appealing to the masses.

アメリカのスタンドアップコメディーに比べて、漫才にはあまり挑発的な内容を追求しない傾向があり、大衆にウケることが優先されています。

Andrew's Point

Even before I had ever set foot in Japan, I knew of Dauntaun. I think in the late 1990s or early 2000s, I must have found an online forum or peer-to-peer site that had a bunch of Dauntaun video clips. And I, like many people in their teens or early twenties at the time, became hooked on *manzai* and the distinctly Japanese—or Kansai?—brand of comedy. Coincidentally, the first place I lived in Japan was Himeji, just a short train ride from Amagasaki, which is where Matsumoto and Hamada are from. Or perhaps it was not a coincidence; maybe it was destiny.

日本に足を踏み入れる前から、私はダウンタウンを知っていました。1990年代後半か2000年代前半に、確か、ダウンタウンの動画が大量に見られるオンラインフォーラムかピアツーピアのサイトを見つけたのです。そして、当時の10代から20代前半の人たちの多くがそうだったように、私も漫才や日本——あるいは関西?——特有のお笑いに夢中になりました。偶然にも、私が日本で最初に住んだ場所は姫路で、松本さんや浜田さんの出身地である尼崎から電車ですぐのところでした。あるいはたぶん、それは偶然ではなく運命だったのかもしれません。

紅白歌合戦

115

Year-End Song Battle
年末歌合戦

文で説明してみよう！

Kōhaku Uta Gassen is a once-popular annual year-end television special featuring a song contest between two teams separated by gender.

紅白歌合戦は、一頃人気が高かった年末恒例のテレビ特番で、男女別の2チームによる歌合戦が行われる。

3語フレーズを会話で使おう！

The musical numbers in the annual **Year-End Song Battle** may appeal to some, but I've never really understood the point of making it into a competition.

毎年の紅白歌合戦で歌われる曲は、一部の人にとっては魅力的かもしれませんが、それを競技形式にする意味が私にはよく理解できません。

Andrew's Point

I may invite some ire with my point here, but I've never understood the point of Kōhaku Uta Gassen. It's presented as a song "battle," but the victors gain nothing. And because there are so many bands and genres, it seems to me that there can't be anyone who likes listening to absolutely every song broadcasted. But year in and year out, people tune in from start to finish and get caught up in the competition. I just don't understand the draw. The most exciting part for me in recent years when I see it playing at my in-law's place is the *kendama* event. Now that's a kind of suspense that can keep me engaged!

こういう話をすると怒りを買うかもしれませんが、私は紅白歌合戦の良さが全く分かりません。歌の「戦い」という体裁を取っていますが、勝者に何の得もありません。それに、あまりにも多くのバンドやジャンルが網羅されているので、何としても放送されるすべての曲を聞きたい、などという人がいるはずはありません。なのに毎年毎年、人々はこの番組を最初から最後まで視聴し、歌合戦のとりこになるのです。私にはその魅力が理解できません。近年、義理の両親の家でこの番組を見て、私が一番面白いと思ったのは、けん玉コーナーです。ああいう種類のワクワク感になら、ずっと没入していられるのですが！

雅楽

imperial court music

宮中音楽

 文で説明してみよう！

Gagaku is the oldest type of music in Japan, and it was historically used at the Imperial court during rituals performed by the Imperial family.

gagaku は日本最古の音楽で、歴史的には宮中で皇室の人たちが営む儀式で用いられていた。

 ３語フレーズを会話で使おう！

Imperial court music bears an unearthly quality, able to hold my attention for hours despite the melodies never forming into solid memories in my mind.

雅楽には不思議な特質があり、メロディーがしっかり記憶に残るわけではないのに、何時間でも没入できるのです。

Andrew's Point

No matter how you describe *gagaku*, be it with three words or three hundred, the only way for someone to understand it is to hear it. Even an in-depth explanation of some of the instruments, such as the bamboo flutes (*ryūteki*, *komabue*, *kagurabue*) or the *biwa* or *kakko* would fail to give any clear impression of the type of music produced. All that aside, I love *gagaku* and can listen to it for hours on end. I find it hauntingly beautiful, an echo of ancient times. I envy those who got to hear it regularly in the Imperial court. I wonder if I lived in Japan in a previous life.

雅楽をどう説明しようと、それが3語であろうと300語であろうと、人に理解してもらうには実際に聞いてもらうしかありません。龍笛や高麗笛、神楽笛、琵琶、鞨鼓など、いくつかの楽器について詳しく説明しても、どんな音楽が奏でられるのか、明確なイメージは伝わらないでしょう。それはともかく、私は雅楽が大好きで、何時間でも聞いていられます。心にしみるほど美しく、古代の響きを感じます。宮中で定期的に聞くことができた人たちをうらやましく思います。私は前世は日本に住んでいたのでしょうか。

蹴鞠

soccer juggling precursor
サッカー式曲芸の先駆者

 文で説明してみよう！

Kemari is a game in which players wearing leather shoes cooperate to keep a leather ball in the air and prevent it from touching the ground using any body part aside from their arms and hands.

蹴鞠とは、鴨沓を履いた参加者たちが協力して、腕と手以外の体のあらゆる部位を使い、革製のまりを空中に浮かせたまま、地面に落とさないようにする遊びである。

 ３語フレーズを会話で使おう！

I marveled at a group of Shintō priests keeping the ball aloft in the **soccer juggling precursor** and wondered if many of the soccer greats could do the same.

神官たちが蹴鞠でまりを浮かせ続けているのに驚嘆した私は、サッカーの名選手の多くが同じことができるのか訝ってしまいました。

Andrew's Point

I've appeared on TV in Japan twice. The first time was in 2010 during a *kemari* event that took place at Shiramine Jingū in Kyoto. I was so excited to be able to participate because I played soccer for many, many years. The Japanese participants all wore traditional garb, and I was impressed at how well they were able to kick the ball around. And then it came to me and… "thud." Someone had to chase it down. I had no idea the ball would be less inflated than a standard soccer ball. I did better on my second attempt, but what a thing to catch on camera.

私は日本で2度テレビに映りました。初回は2010年、京都の白峯神宮で行われた蹴鞠のイベントでした。参加できるとあって、私はとても興奮しました。とても長い間サッカーをやっていたからです。日本人の参加者は皆、伝統的な装束を身に着けており、私は彼らが実に上手にまりを蹴って回せることに感銘を受けました。やがて、まりが私のところに来て……「ドサッ」。誰かが追いかけるはめに陥りました。まりが普通のサッカーボールほど膨らんでいないとは思いもよらなかったのです。2回目の挑戦ではうまくいきましたが、カメラに収められてしまうとは。

118

スタジオジブリ
Feature-Length Anime Studio
長編アニメ製作会社

🗨 *Sutajio Ghibli* is an internationally acclaimed animation studio with more than twenty feature-length films to its name.

スタジオジブリは、国際的に高く評価されているアニメーション製作会社で、20本を超える長編作品を同社名で発表している。

💬 Watching a **Feature-Length Anime Studio** film, I can't help but feel "spirited away" to another universe.

スタジオジブリの映画を見ていると、どうしても別の宇宙へ「神隠しされた」ような気分になるのです。

※ Spirited Away はスタジオジブリの作品『千と千尋の神隠し』の英題。

相撲
wrestling of mountains 山たちのレスリング

🗨 *Sumō*, Japan's national sport, is an ancient form of wrestling whereby a contestant loses if any part of his body aside from his feet touches the ground or if he is forced out of a designated ring.

相撲は日本の国技で、レスリングの古い形式の一つである。両方の足以外の体の部位が地面に触れたり、決められた輪の外へ押し出されたりすると負けとなる。

💬 The uninitiated may consider **wrestling of mountains** the violent clashing of tectonic behemoths, but in truth, it is a delicate art form with the grace of ballet.

詳しくない人は、相撲が地殻を揺るがすほどの巨体の激しいぶつかり合いだと考えるかもしれませんが、実際にはバレエのような優美さを持った繊細な芸能なのです。

落語
comic monologue storytelling こっけいな1人話

Rakugo, literally translated as "fallen words," is a type of comedic monologue featuring a lone storyteller clad in a kimono kneeling atop a cushion and holding only a fan and hand towel as props.

落語は、直訳すると「落ちた言葉」で、1人で語るこっけい話の一種。1人の話者が着物を着て座布団の上に膝をつき、扇子と手ぬぐいだけを小道具として持つ。

As **comic monologue storytelling** embraces globalization and more speakers of languages aside from Japanese take up the art form, I wonder whether **comic monologue storytelling** artists will come to be recognized as "sit-down comics" in contrast to the popular "stand-up comics" typical in the West.

落語がグローバル化し、日本語以外の言語を話す落語家が増えれば、欧米で一般的な「スタンドアップコメディアン」に対して「シットダウンコメディアン」として落語家が認知されるようになるのでしょうか。

歌舞伎
highly stylized dance-drama 高度に様式化された舞踏劇

Kabuki is a traditional performance art featuring glamorous costumes, distinctive makeup, music, and dance.

歌舞伎は伝統芸能の一つで、華やかな衣装、独特の化粧と音楽、踊りが特徴である。

Highly stylized dance-drama may be a traditional art form, but these days, it can be found with the trappings of modern technologies like projection mapping.

歌舞伎は伝統的な芸術形態かもしれませんが、最近ではプロジェクションマッピングのような現代的な技術を取り入れたものも見られます。

119

文楽
traditional puppet theater 伝統的な人形劇

Bunraku is a traditional form of Japanese puppet theater using half-life-sized stringless puppets and rhythmic chanting accompanied by music to tell a story.

文楽は日本の伝統的な人形劇で、実寸の半分のサイズの、操りひもがない人形を使い、音楽に合わせてリズミカルに詠唱しながら物語を伝えるもの。

I didn't take puppet theater seriously until I saw a **traditional puppet theater** performance and ended up bawling my eyes out.

文楽の公演を見て最後に涙を流してしまうまで、私は人形劇をばかにしていました。

演歌
traditional balladic music 伝統的なバラード調音楽

Enka is a genre of music that makes use of pentatonic scales and *kobushi*, a type of melismatic vocal technique, and the songs often describe heartbreak or tragedy.

演歌は、5音音階と、こぶしというメリスマ様式＊の歌唱技術を駆使する音楽ジャンルで、失恋や悲劇を歌った曲が多い。

It must have been quite a shock when, at 2:00 a.m. in the dusky bar tucked into a Himeji alleyway, the lone foreigner started crooning his favorite **traditional balladic music** on the ancient *karaoke* machine.

午前2時、姫路の路地にひっそりとたたずむ薄暗いバーで、その外国人の一人客が古びたカラオケマシンを使ってお気に入りの演歌を甘く歌い始めたときの衝撃は、相当なものだったに違いありません。

＊歌詞の1音節に多数の音符を当てて装飾的に歌う声楽の様式

三味線
three-stringed traditional banjo
3弦の伝統的なバンジョー

The *shamisen* is a long-necked, three-stringed fretless lute played with one of a variety of large plectrums to achieve different sounds.

三味線は、棹の長い3弦のフレットがないリュートで、さまざまな大型のばちを使って多様な音を出す。

The **three-stringed traditional banjo**, while a traditional instrument, has enjoyed a revival of sorts as it has found its way into rock music.

三味線は伝統的な楽器でありながら、ロック音楽に取り入れられて、ある種の復活を遂げています。

三線
snakeskin-covered Okinawan banjo
ヘビ革で覆われた沖縄のバンジョー

The precursor to the *shamisen*, the *sanshin* is a three-stringed musical instrument akin to a banjo and comprised of a neck, body, and pegs.

三味線の前身である三線は、バンジョーに似た3弦の楽器で、棹、胴、糸巻きで構成されている。

My heart rejoices when the cheerful twang of the **snakeskin-covered Okinawan banjo** imbues the air with Okinawan soul.

三線の陽気な響きが空気に沖縄の魂を吹き込むと、私はうれしくなります。

120

尺八
bamboo end-blown flute
竹製の先端吹き込み式フルート

🗒 A *shakuhachi* is a traditional end-blown flute predominantly made of bamboo.

尺八は、主に竹で作られた伝統的な先端吹き込み式フルートである。

💬 For some people, a **bamboo end-blown flute** is simply an instrument among many, but for me, it resurrects the voice of ancient Japan.

尺八を、単に数ある楽器のうちの一つに過ぎないと捉える人もいますが、私にとっては大昔の日本の声をよみがえらせてくれるものです。

太鼓
Japanese percussion instruments 日本の打楽器

🗒 *Taiko*, like "drum," describes a broad range of percussion instruments.

太鼓は、drumと同様に、幅広い種類の打楽器を指す言葉。

💬 As I passed the 20-kilometer marker in the marathon, a **Japanese percussion instruments** ensemble lent wings to my stride, urging me forward with a thunderous beat.

マラソンで20キロ地点を通過したところで、太鼓の合奏による応援のおかげで私の足運びは羽が生えたように軽やかになり、とどろくビートが私を前へ押し出してくれました。

でんでん太鼓
two-headed pellet drum 2面小球付き太鼓

🔵 A ***den-den daiko*** is a two-headed drum suspended on a rod with beads or pellets hanging from cords on both sides.

でんでん太鼓は、打面が2つある太鼓を棒に取り付けたもので、両方の打面に小球が結び付けられている。

💬 I'm sure my son enjoyed the **two-headed pellet drum** he was given by his nursery school, but his baby sister—who was trying to sleep when he returned home with it—surely did not.

間違いなく息子は保育園からもらってきたでんでん太鼓を
楽しんでいましたが、息子の幼い妹——息子の帰宅時に眠
りかけていました——は、絶対に楽しめなかったはずです。

琵琶
short-necked wooden lute 棹の短い木製リュート

🔵 The ***biwa*** is a short-necked, wooden lute with a pear-shaped body and silk strings.

琵琶は、棹の短い木製のリュートで、洋ナシの形をした胴に絹の弦を張ったものである。

💬 The resounding buzz of the strings hitting the hard neck of the **short-necked wooden lute** pierced the concert hall, demanding the attention of the audience.

琵琶の硬い棹に弦がぶつかるブンブンという音がコンサートホールに響き渡り、
いやおうなく聴衆の注意を引き付けました。

121

箏

plucked half-tube zither 撥弦半管チター

The *koto*, which is the national instrument of Japan, is a plucked half-tube zither with 13 silk strings and movable bridges.

箏は日本の伝統楽器で、13本の絹の弦と可動式の箏柱を備えた撥弦半管チターである。

The **plucked half-tube zither** is sometimes referred to as the Japanese harp, but I think it produces a wider range of expression than an actual harp.

箏は日本のハープと呼ばれることもありますが、本物のハープよりも幅広い表現ができると思います。

Chapter

9

Education/School Life

教育・学校

ランドセル

122

Dutch-inspired school backpack

オランダ由来の学校用バックパック

 文で説明してみよう！

Randoseru, adopted from "ransel," the Dutch word for backpack, are hard-backed school bags typically made from leather or a leather-like synthetic.

ランドセルは、バックパックを意味するオランダ語のranselに由来し、通常、革または合成皮革で作られた裏地の硬い通学かばんである。

 ３語フレーズを会話で使おう！

Foreigners with no understanding of Japanese history would likely find it strange and amusing that **Dutch-inspired school backpacks** are the norm in Japan.

日本史がまったく分からない外国人は、ランドセルが日本で標準となっていることを不思議に思い、面白がるでしょう。

Andrew's Point

Regardless of the expression I chose for this one, I think a picture will be necessary to make it clear to someone. While "Dutch-inspired school backpack" is perfectly accurate, what "Dutch-inspired" means will depend very much on the listener. Some people have no knowledge of The Netherlands beyond the iconic windmills, so I imagine people might believe all *randoseru* to have propellers rotating serenely in the wind as students skip along on their way to school.

この言葉に該当する英語表現としてどんなものを選ぶにしろ、分かりやすく伝えるためには写真が必要になるだろうと思います。**Dutch-inspired school backpack** という表現は正確ですが、**Dutch-inspired** が何を意味するかは、聞く人によって大きく変わってきます。象徴である風車以外、オランダについて何も知らない人もいるので、こんなふうに思う人がいても不思議はないと想像します。ランドセルはにはどれもプロペラが付いていて、生徒たちがスキップしながら通学する途中で、風に吹かれてプロペラが静かに回転するのではないかと。

予備校

exam-focussed college-preparatory school
入試に特化した大学準備学校

 文で説明してみよう！

Yobikō are privately run schools that prepare students for entrance examinations for admissions to higher institutions of learning.

予備校は私立の学校で、生徒に上位教育機関への入学試験を受ける準備をさせる。

 3語フレーズを会話で使おう！

Knowing he would ultimately end up working at his father's company, Shinichirō figured that attending an **exam-focused college-preparatory school** would be a waste of time and money.

最終的には父親の会社で働くことになると分かっていたので、シンイチロウは予備校などに通うのは時間とお金の無駄だと考えました。

Andrew's Point

The number of people in the U.S. who understand the idea of an "exam-focussed college-preparatory school" might be dwindling. The reason is that many colleges and graduate schools are dropping the requirement of any sort of overarching academic assessment, choosing instead to rely on other means of student evaluation. In Finland, there is a Matriculation Examination undergone toward the end of high school. Passing it is a requirement for completing the Finnish upper secondary school, and the scores play a significant role in university admissions. Despite that, however, Finnish schools have such a comprehensive and balanced approach that there is no market for *yobikō* (Some students do seek private tutoring, however).

アメリカでは、「予備校」を設けるという発想を理解する人が減っているかもしれません。理由は、多くの大学や大学院が包括的な学力評価試験を課さなくなっており、代わりに他の手段で学生を評価することを選んでいることにあります。フィンランドでは、高校卒業前に大学入試が実施されます。これに合格することは、フィンランドで高校を卒業するための必須条件であり、そのスコアは大学入学時に重要な役割を果たします。にもかかわらず、フィンランドの学校は極めて総合的でバランスの取れた教育を行っているため、予備校の市場は存在しません（ただし、個人教授を求める生徒はいます）。

就職活動

end-of-college job-hunting activities

大学終盤の求職活動

 文で説明してみよう！

Shūshoku katsudō describes the job-hunting activities performed by third-year and fourth-year university students.

就職活動とは、大学3、4年生が行う求職活動のことである。

 ３語フレーズを会話で使おう！

While all my friends were stressed out about their **end-of-college job-hunting activities**, I could rest easy as I had been hired directly by a company I had interned for over the summer.

友人たちが皆、就職活動で疲弊している中、私はのんびりできました。夏にインターンをしていた会社に直接採用されていたからです。

Andrew's Point

The concept of "end-of-college job-hunting activities" in Japan shares some similarities with the career development and job recruitment processes in the U.S., such as having career counselors and companies conducting on-campus interviews, but there are also significant differences in terms of structure, timeline, and cultural expectations. The U.S. job-hunting process is generally less formalized, and there is more variability in the timeline for securing employment post-graduation. Campus recruiting does occur, but not all companies adhere to the same hiring schedule, and there is more emphasis on individual hiring rather than group hiring of new graduates. Additionally, the U.S. process typically places a higher emphasis on individuality, both in terms of job-hunting attire and in the application process, with customized resumes and cover letters being the norm. In other words, there are no "job interview suits."

日本における就職活動には、キャリアカウンセラーの存在や企業による学内面接など、アメリカのキャリア形成や採用のプロセスと共通する部分もありますが、仕組みやスケジュール、社会的に求められていること、といった点では大きな違いがあります。米国の求職活動のプロセスは一般的に形式化されておらず、卒業後の雇用へ向けた採用スケジュールにはより大きなばらつきがあります。大学生相手の採用活動は行われますが、すべての企業が同じ採用スケジュールに従うわけではなく、新卒者の集団採用よりも個人採用に重点が置かれます。加えて、アメリカでの採用プロセスでは、一般的に個性が非常に重視されます。それは、求職活動中の服装にも応募プロセスにおいてもです。応募者独自の履歴書やカバーレターを作成するのが標準で、「リクルートスーツ」はありません。

中高一貫教育

combined secondary school

複合中等学校

文で説明してみよう！

Chūkō ikkan kyōiku is an integrated junior high school and high school whereby students advance directly from one school to the next, usually without having to pass an entrance examination.

中高一貫教育とは、中学校と高校が統合された形態のことで、そこでは生徒たちが、通常、入試に合格するという工程を経ずにそのまま進学する。

３語フレーズを会話で使おう！

Riku could have had it easy getting into high school because he attended a **combined secondary school**, but he really wanted to be on the baseball team at a different high school across town.

リクは中高一貫校に通っていたので、難なく高校に進学できたはずなのですが、町の反対側にある別の高校へ行き、どうしてもそこの野球部に入りたいと思いました。

Andrew's Point

The idea of a "combined secondary school" will make sense to many Westerners. Indeed, similar schools exist in the U.S. There are also K-12 schools in the U.S., where students can attend the same school from kindergarten through the final year of high school. But those don't exist where I grew up. Education in the U.S. is extremely variable when it comes to both school composition and curriculum. There are laws and guidance provided at the federal level by the Department of Education, standards and policies set by state Departments of Education, school districts organized at the city or county level operated by school boards, which are usually elected by the local community, and then the schools themselves that have some flexibility within the framework set by all the powers above them. The result is, unfortunately, a huge mess in many cases.

「中高一貫教育」という考え方は、多くの欧米人にとって理にかなったものでしょう。事実、アメリカにも同様の学校があります。アメリカには、幼稚園から高校の最終学年までつながっているK-12学校というものもあります。ただし、私が育った場所にはそういう学校はありません。アメリカの教育では、学校の構成もカリキュラムも極めて多様です。教育省による連邦レベルでの法律や指導、州の教育局による基準や方針、ふつう地域の住民によって選出される教育委員会が運営する市や郡レベルの学区、そして、こうしたあらゆる権限の下に設定された枠組みの中で一定の柔軟性を持つ学校そのものがあります。結果的に、残念ながら多くの場合、大混乱に陥るのです。

浪人

entrance exam retaker

入試再受験者

文で説明してみよう！

While historical *rōnin* were masterless samurai during Japan's feudal period, today's *rōnin* are students who failed their university entrance exams and are studying for a year or years to take them again.

歴史上の浪人は、日本の封建時代に主君を持たない武士のことだったが、今日の浪人とは、大学受験に失敗し、再受験のために1年間かそれ以上勉強している学生のことである。

3語フレーズを会話で使おう！

I was worried Nao had become a socially withdrawn shut-in, but in actuality she was dead set on getting into the University of Tokyo as an **entrance exam retaker**.

私はナオが引きこもりになったのではないかと心配しましたが、実は浪人して東大に入ることを固く決意していたのです。

Andrew's Point

The idea of an "entrance exam retaker" is not completely foreign to people in the West. In the U.S., students often retake the SAT or ACT, two prominent college admissions tests, multiple times to try to get a better score. However, it's relatively unusual for a student to graduate high school and continue such testing. In the U.K., students take A-Levels, which are two-year courses that culminate with an exam at the end of each year. The grades on their A-Level exams directly impact their university admission prospects, so in some cases, students will take an additional year to study and retake the exams.

「浪人」というコンセプトは、欧米の人々にとって全くなじみがないわけでもありません。アメリカでは、生徒たちが大学入学共通テストとして有名なSATやACTを何度も受け直し、より良いスコアの獲得を目指すことがよくあります。しかし、高校を卒業してからもこの種のテストを受け続ける生徒は、比較的珍しいのです。イギリスでは、生徒たちはAレベルという2年間のコースを履修し、各年の終わりに試験を受けます。Aレベルの試験の成績は大学進学に直接影響するので、場合によってはさらに1年間勉強して再受験します。

127

運動会
school-wide sports festival 全校スポーツ祭

🔖 *Undōkai* is a field day or sports festival staged by schools, offices, or local communities.

運動会とは、学校や職場、地域社会が主催する体育大会の日または体育祭のこと。

💬 The kindergarten **school-wide sports festival** teetered on the verge of chaos, but everyone seemed to enjoy themselves.

幼稚園の運動会は混乱寸前の状態でしたが、みんな楽しそうでした。

体操着
school gym clothes 学校の体育用着衣

🔖 *Taisōgi*, literally translated as "gym clothes," are the clothes used by school students in gym class, typically kept at school in a designated gym clothes bag that is brought home to clean every Friday.

体操着は、直訳すると「体育用の服」で、学校の生徒が体育の授業で着用する服である。通常、決められた体操着袋に入れて学校で保管し、毎週金曜日に家へ持ち帰って洗濯する。

💬 Chie couldn't understand how her son managed to come home every Friday with his **school gym clothes** completely caked in mud.

チエは、自分の息子が毎週金曜日に、泥がこびりついた体操着をよくも平気で持ち帰れるものだと思いました。

遠足
school field trip 学校の校外学習

Ensoku are school field trips taken by students in kindergarten, elementary school, and junior high school to such places as parks, the seaside, or the mountains.

遠足とは、幼稚園や小中学校の園児・児童・生徒たちが出かける校外学習のことで、公園や海辺、山などの場所を訪れる。

My oldest son couldn't contain his excitement when he learned that his kindergarten class was headed to a local park for a **school field trip**.

私の長男は、幼稚園のクラスの遠足で地元の公園に行くと知って、興奮を抑えきれませんでした。

学芸会
school arts festival 学校の芸術祭

Gakugeikai is a school event where mainly elementary school students perform a variety of musical and theatrical productions to demonstrate their learning.

学芸会は学校行事で、主に小学生がさまざまな音楽や演劇の演目をこなし、学習の成果を披露する。

We were amazed when we heard Takako singing at the **school arts festival**, and we knew that she was destined for stardom.

学芸会でタカコの歌声を聞いた私たちは驚き、あの子はきっとスターダムにのし上がるだろうと確信しました。

文化祭
school cultural exhibition 学校の文化展示会

128

Bunkasai are school "culture festivals" wherein students can show off their skills and knowledge in a variety of ways to their teachers, peers, and, in many cases, the public.

文化祭とは、学校の「文化の祭り」のことで、生徒たちが自分の技能や知識をさまざまな形で教師や同級生、そして多くの場合、一般の人たちに披露する。

The dance routines and musical numbers at the **school cultural exhibition** were certainly impressive, but I couldn't believe some of the magnificent chalkboard drawings were drawn by mere high school students.

文化祭でのダンスの演目や音楽の演奏は確かに印象的でしたが、私が信じられなかったのは、あの壮大な黒板アートのいくつかが、一介の高校生たちが描いたものだったということです。

大学入学共通テスト
General Admission Examination 共通入学試験

The *Daigakunyūgaku Kyōtsū Tesuto* is a standardized entrance examination used by universities across Japan.

大学入学共通テストは、日本全国の大学で採用されている統一入学試験である。

When the **General Admission Examination** superseded the previous test, many of the old study materials that stocked the shelves of bookstores became practically worthless.

大学入学共通テストが旧試験に取って代わると、書店に並んでいた古い教材の多くが事実上、無価値になってしまいました。

センター試験
Nationwide Standardized Examination
全国標準試験

The **Sentā Shiken** was a standardized university entrance exam used by universities, both public and private, throughout Japan until 2020, when it was superseded by the *Daigakunyūgaku Kyōtsū Tesuto*.

センター試験は、2020年に大学入学共通テストに取って代わられるまで、国公立・私立を問わず全国の大学で採用されていた統一大学入学試験である。

While the **Nationwide Standardized Examination** and its successor are pivotal with regard to determining one's future in Japan, there is a trend in America to deemphasize testing in favor of more holistic means of student assessment.

センター試験とその後継試験は、日本では人の将来を決定する上でとても重要なものですが、アメリカでは試験に重きを置かず、より総合的な方法で生徒を評価する方向に傾いています。

大学入試センター
University Examination Authority 大学入試当局

The **Daigakunyūshi Sentā** is the institution under the Ministry of Education, Culture, Sports, Science and Technology that is responsible for administering the *Daigakunyūgaku Kyōtsū Tesuto* and law school entrance exams in Japan.

大学入試センターは、文部科学省の下部機関で、日本の大学入学共通テストや法科大学院入試を管轄する。

Looking at the results of her entrance exam, Mio cursed the **University Examination Authority** and prepared for her life as a *rōnin*.

自分の入試の結果を見て、ミオは大学入試センターを呪い、浪人生活に備えました。

学習塾
supplementary exam-prep school
補習と試験準備の学校

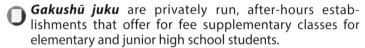 *Gakushū juku* are privately run, after-hours establishments that offer for fee supplementary classes for elementary and junior high school students.

学習塾とは、私立の放課後に運営される教育施設で、小中学生を対象に有料で補習授業を行う。

Bored at the **supplementary exam-prep school**, Maya couldn't help but daydream about moving to Finland, where going to school from morning to night was practically unheard of.

学習塾で退屈したマヤは、思わず空想にふけってしまいました。朝から晩まで学校に通うことなど考えられないフィンランドに引っ越す、という空想でした。

六三三制
school division system 学校の区分け制度

Rokusansansei, literally translated as "6-3-3 system," describes the primary and secondary school system whereby students attend elementary school for six years, junior high school for three years, and high school for three years.

六三三制は、直訳すると「6・3・3制度」で、小学校に6年間、中学校に3年間、高校に3年間通うという初等および中等教育の制度のことである。

When Yumiko moved to America, she was surprised to learn that not only do they not have a system like **school division system**, but also that some schools, even in the same city, have different systems from one another.

アメリカに引っ越したユミコが知って驚いたのは、六三三制のような制度がないばかりか、同じ市内でも学校によって制度が違うことでした。

Chapter
10

Expressions
表現・言い回し

「いただきます」

"Let us eat."

「さあ食べましょう」

 文で説明してみよう！

"Itadakimasu." is a polite expression offered immediately before a meal to convey one's appreciation for all of the people who were involved in the production of the meal, from farmers to butchers to chefs to parents.

「いただきます」は、食事の直前に口に出される丁寧な表現で、農家から精肉業者、料理人、両親に至るまで、料理を作ることに関わったすべての人への感謝の気持ちを伝えるもの。

 3語フレーズを会話で使おう！

Sakura's mom had barely finished saying **"Let us eat."** before Sakura's cheeks were completely stuffed with *takoyaki*.

母親が「いただきます」を言い終わらないうちに、サクラはたこ焼きを口一杯にほおばっていました。

Andrew's Point

While Westerners aren't alien to the idea of being thankful, pre-meal expressions of gratitude are typically limited to religious ones, such as saying "Grace." in Christianity, reciting the "Motzi." in Judaism, or uttering "Bismillah." in Islam. Because "Itadakimasu." is a secular expression, I opted to avoid translating it as "Let's say Grace." or any equivalent associated with specific religious traditions. Given that "Itadakimasu." is considered polite, I also steered clear of more casual expressions like "Let's dig in." (natural albeit casual) or "Ready, set, eat!" (humorous and unusual). Ultimately, "Let us eat" seemed to carry the solemnity of a religious expression without being encumbered by any actual religious affiliations.

欧米人が感謝を知らないわけではありませんが、食前の感謝の表現は、宗教的なものに限られています。キリスト教では Grace. と言い、ユダヤ教では Motzi. と唱え、イスラム教では Bismillah. を口にします。「いただきます」は非宗教的な表現であるため、Let's say Grace. などと訳したり、特定の宗教的伝統に関わる同様の表現を使ったりすることは避けました。「いただきます」は丁寧な表現だと見なされているので、Let's dig in. (自然だがくだけている) や Ready, set, eat! (ユーモラスであまり使われない) のようなよりカジュアルな表現も外しました。結局、Let us eat. が、現実の宗教の色にじゃまされずに、宗教的な表現が持つ厳粛さを伝えられるように思えたのです。

「ごちそうさま」

"Great meal, thanks!"

「素晴らしい食事をありがとう！」

 文で説明してみよう！

"Gochisōsama." is the expression used after a meal to convey appreciation to those involved with making the meal, such as a cook, a farmer, a fisherman, or one's parents.

「ごちそうさま」は食後に使われる表現で、調理師や農家、漁師、両親など、料理を作ることに関わった人たちに感謝の気持ちを伝えるもの。

 3語フレーズを会話で使おう！

Ami was impressed that whenever her daughter's best friend came over for dinner, she always finished the meal by saying, **"Great meal, thanks!"**

アミが感銘を受けたのは、娘の親友が夕食を食べに来るたびに、「ごちそうさま」と言って食事を終えることでした。

Andrew's Point

I distinctly remember an episode from when I was in elementary school. Out of hearing range of my mother, who cooked for us each and every day, my father told me and my two siblings, "From now on, you need to thank your mother for every meal. It's a lot of work, and you shouldn't take it for granted." He was right. There was no *gochisōsama*-like tradition in our home, just like in many other homes. But there really should be. "Great meal, thanks." fits the bill. You could also say, "Loved every bite." or "Satisfying and delicious," but that might come across as disingenuous if you don't actually feel that way.

小学生の頃のある出来事を、はっきり覚えています。毎日欠かさず食事を用意してくれている母の耳の届かないところで、父が私と2人のきょうだいに言ったのです。「これからは、毎食お母さんに感謝しなさい。大変な仕事なんだから、それを当たり前だと思ってはいけない」と。父の言うとおりでした。わが家には、ごちそうさまのような言葉を交わす習慣はありませんでした。それは、他の多くの家庭でも同じでした。でも、本当はあるべきなのです。**Great meal, thanks.** ならぴったりです。他に、**Loved every bite.**（一口一口がとてもおいしかった）あるいは**Satisfying and delicious.**（十分な量で、おいしかった）などと言うこともできますが、これらは、本当にそう感じていない場合、不誠実だと受け取られる可能性があります。

「おじゃまします」

132

"Pardon my intrusion."

「立ち入ることを許してください」

文で説明してみよう！

"Ojamashimasu," literally translated as "I will disturb you," is the expression used as a polite greeting when entering someone's home.

「おじゃまします」は、直訳すると「私はあなたをじゃまします」で、人の家に入るときの丁寧な挨拶として使われる表現である。

3語フレーズを会話で使おう！

When Hiroki walked into the unfamiliar apartment, he reflexively said **"pardon my intrusion"** before remembering that he now lived there.

ヒロキは、まだ不慣れなアパートに足を踏み入れて、反射的に「おじゃまします」と言ってしまってから、自分が今そこに住んでいることを思い出しました。

Andrew's Point

In the West, as in Japan, ordinarily you ask for permission before entering a room (e.g., "May I come in?"). But unlike in the West, in Japan, even after receiving permission, you then offer forgiveness for the intrusion you present by entering the room. This is one of many reasons foreigners are in awe of the Japanese brand of politeness. That said, "Pardon the intrusion." wouldn't be completely unnatural in a Western setting; it would just be unusually polite. As an aside, I like the versatility of the word "jama." With three young kids from Kansai, I hear "Jama sentoite!" and "Jama sunna!" about 100 times a day. There's a whole world of difference between "Pardon my intrusion." and "Get the f*ck out of my way!"

欧米でも、日本と同様に、部屋に入る前には許可を求めます（例えば**May I come in?** と言って）。しかし、欧米と違って日本では、許可を得た後でもさらに、入室によって相手のじゃまをすることに許しを請うのです。これは、外国人が日本特有の礼儀正しさに畏敬の念を抱く数多くの理由の一つです。とはいえ、欧米社会で**Pardon the intrusion.**（おじゃまをお許しください）と言ったところで、全く不自然というわけではありません。ただ、異常に丁寧になるでしょうが。余談ですが、私は「じゃま」という言葉の汎用性を気に入っています。関西生まれの子供が3人いるので、「じゃませんといて！」や「じゃますんな！」を日に100回くらい聞きます。「おじゃまします」と「じゃますんな！」は天と地ほど違いますね。

「お世話になります」

133

"Appreciate the support."

「お手伝いに感謝します」

 文で説明してみよう！

"Osewa ni narimasu." is a phrase used to express appreciation for someone's ongoing or future work or service.

「お世話になります」は、誰かの現在または未来の仕事や奉仕に対して感謝の意を表すために使われるフレーズである。

 ３語フレーズを会話で使おう！

Upon their first meeting, Sarah said **"Appreciate the support."** to her host sister, resulting in a smile of surprise and delight.

初対面のとき、サラがホストシスターに「お世話になります」と言うと、驚きと喜びの笑顔が帰ってきました。

Andrew's Point

Here we get to a pair of expressions that are confusing without deep cultural understanding and context: "Osewa ni narimasu." and "Yoroshiku onegaishimasu." To a non-native speaker, they feel very similar: both are expressions of appreciation for future care or support. Indeed, "Thanks in advance." (used for the next "Yoroshiku onegaishimasu.") is one option here. But I thought to differentiate them as this expression, to me, seems a little more limited in scope than the all-encompassing "Yoroshiku onegaishimasu." "Appreciate the support" also feels more fitting at the start of an email than "Thanks in advance," which would do better at the end of an email. In addition, it's important to note that lacking an initial I ("I appreciate the support.") makes it sound somewhat informal.

ここで、深い文化的理解と文脈抜きでは混乱する2つの表現を見てみましょう。「お世話になります」と「よろしくお願いします」です。日本語の非ネイティブスピーカーには、この2つは酷似しているように感じられます。いずれも、これから受けるであろう世話や援助に対する感謝の表現です。確かに、（次項の「よろしくお願いします」で用いた）Thanks in advance. も、「お世話になります」に当てる選択肢の一つです。しかし、私はこの2つを区別しようと考えました。この「お世話になります」は、私には、包括的な「よろしくお願いします」よりも少し範囲が限定されているように思えるからです。Appreciate the support. はまた、Thanks in advance. よりもメールの冒頭で使うとしっくりきます。Thanks in advance. は、メールの最後に置くほうがいいのです。それから、主語のI（I appreciate the support. のI）を省いたことで、いくぶんくだけた印象を与える点も、念頭に置く必要があります。

「よろしくお願いします」

134

"Thanks in advance."

「あらかじめ感謝します」

文で説明してみよう！

"Yoroshiku onegai shimasu." is an expression used when expecting service, kindness, or support.

「よろしくお願いします」は、サービスや親切、援助を期待しているときに使われる表現である。

３語フレーズを会話で使おう！

Jennifer found during her time in Japan that many barriers crumbled away with ease just by saying, **"Thanks in advance."**

ジェニファーは日本に滞在中に、「よろしくお願いします」と言うだけで多くの障害を乗り越えられることに気づきました。

Andrew's Point

I've heard a lot of bad attempts at translations of "Yoroshiku onegaishimasu." One common one that I always shake my head at is "Please treat me kindly." As if you would otherwise expect me to treat you unkindly. There's also "I look forward to working with you." This translation is acceptable, but only for a specific situation—it doesn't make any sense when you're dropping your kids off at kindergarten. "Thanks in advance." covers most situations that I can think of and captures the essence of the phrase. You're showing that you're grateful for some service, activity, or courtesy that you expect performed at some point or during some period in the future.

私は「よろしくお願いします」の英訳の失敗例をたくさん耳にしてきました。よくある例で、いつも首を横に振ってしまうのが **Please treat me kindly.** です。まるで、そう言わなければ不親切に扱われそうだ、と言わんばかりです。また、**I look forward to working with you.** というのもあります。この訳は使えますが、限られた状況でのみ有効なものです——子供を幼稚園に送っていったときには役に立ちません。**Thank you in advance.** は、私が思いつけるほとんどの場面をカバーしており、このフレーズの本質を捉えています。未来のある時点または期間に期待するサービスや行動、厚遇に対して感謝していることを伝えていることになるのです。

「お疲れさまでした」

135

"I appreciate you."

「あなたに感謝します」

 文で説明してみよう！

"Otsukaresama deshita," literally translated as "respectfully tired," is a phrase that expresses appreciation for the effort that went into a task.

「お疲れさまでした」は、直訳すれば「疲れていることに敬意を表して」で、課題に払われた努力に対して感謝の意を表明するフレーズである。

 ３語フレーズを会話で使おう！

After her husband successfully put her twin toddlers to bed and plodded wearily into the living room, Maya greeted him by saying, **"I appreciate you."**

夫が幼い双子の子供たちを寝かしつけ、ぐったりして居間に戻ってくると、マヤは彼に「お疲れさまでした」と声をかけました。

Andrew's Point

When I'm in the U.S., it's painfully difficult to live without an English equivalent of "Otsukaresama deshita." When I was in grad school in 2016–2017, I worked on a lot of group projects. After a long day of work, I always wanted to say, "Otsukaresama deshita." to my groupmates. But there was no culturally equivalent way to express my appreciation for their work, so it often ended with a bland, "Well, see you tomorrow!" This linguistic longing feels similar to the emptiness I experience when I sneeze in Japan. It's like my heart is screaming for someone to say, "Bless you!" In the U.S., this custom is so deeply ingrained that if you are on a crowded bus and you sneeze, you're almost guaranteed to hear "Bless you!" being yelled out from some anonymous voice on the other side of the bus.

アメリカにいると、生活する上で「お疲れさまでした」に相当する英語がないことをつらく感じます。2016年から2017年にかけて大学院にいた私は、たくさんのグループプロジェクトに取り組んでいました。長い一日の活動が終わると、私はいつもグループメイトに「お疲れさまでした」と言いたくなりました。しかし、アメリカ文化にはこれに相当する手立てがなく、彼らの取り組みに対する感謝の気持ちを表現できなかったので、たいていは **Well, see you tomorrow!** という当たり障りのない言葉で済ませました。こうした言葉の欠乏感は、日本でくしゃみをしたときに味わうむなしさに似ています。誰かに **Bless you!** と言ってほしいという私の心の叫びに似ているのです。アメリカにはこの習慣が深く根付いていて、混雑したバスの中でくしゃみをすれば、必ずと言っていいほど車内の反対側から、誰とも知れぬ人の **Bless you!** という大声が聞こえます。

「つまらないものですが」

136

"It's nothing much."

「全く大したものではありません」

文で説明してみよう！

"Tsumaranai mono desu ga." is an expression of humility used when offering a gift, and it translates to "Here's a little something I got for you."

「つまらないものですが」は、贈り物をするときに使う謙遜の表現で、「ちょっとしたものをあなたのために用意したので、どうぞ」という意味である。

3語フレーズを会話で使おう！

"It's nothing much," my neighbor said while handing me a jar of homemade jam after I helped her weed her garden.

「つまらないものですが」と隣人が言って、庭の草むしりを手伝ってあげた私に自家製のジャムの瓶を渡してくれました。

Andrew's Point

It goes without saying that all of the terms in this book are somehow Japanese, but this one feels especially Japanese to me. I remember a few months after I moved to Japan, I wanted to give a gift to the manager of a café because of all of the kindness (and free sweets) she had offered me. I can't remember what gift I gave her, but my friend suggested that I say, "Tsumaranai mono desu ga." when I handed the gift over, downplaying my feelings with "tsumaranai." This sort of humility is not something I see so often outside of Japan. In the U.S. in particular, I'd expect something closer to "I really think you're going to like this" or, if someone is expressing a little more humility, "I hope you like this."

言うまでもなく、本書で取り上げたすべての言葉は、何らかの意味で日本的なものです。とはいえ、この表現は私にとってとりわけ日本的に感じられます。日本に引っ越した数カ月後、いろいろ世話になった（そして、ただでお菓子を出してくれた）カフェの店長さんに何か贈り物をしたいと思いました。どんな贈り物をしたかは思い出せないのですが、友人に、贈り物を渡すときには「つまらないものですが」と言えと教えられました。「つまらない」で気持ちを謙遜するのだと。このような謙遜は、日本以外ではあまり聞きません。アメリカでは特に、次のような言葉が予想されます。**I really think you're going to like this.**（絶対にあなたならこれを気に入ると思う）とか、もう少し謙遜するのであれば**I hope you like this.**（これを気に入ってくれるといいけど）などでしょう。

「どうぞ」

137

"Go right ahead."

「そのまま進んで」

 文で説明してみよう！

"Dōzo." is a polite expression meaning that someone should go first, whether it be to pass through a door or start a meal.

「どうぞ」は丁寧な表現で、相手が先行すべきであることを表す。ドアを通り抜ける場合にも食事を始める場合にも使える。

 3語フレーズを会話で使おう！

"Go right ahead," Rensei said, stepping aside to allow me to lead the way down the lantern-lit path of the serene garden.

「どうぞ」とレンセイは言って脇によけ、私に、ちょうちんの明かりが照らす静かな庭の小道を先に進ませてくれました。

Andrew's Point

There are two situations that I struggled to capture here: giving someone permission to proceed, such as through a doorway, and giving someone permission to take something, such as food. I was on the fence between "Go right ahead." and "Please go ahead." because just adding "please" to a two-word expression seems like a violation of the rules of the three-word game. Ultimately, I decided that "Go right ahead." was a good solution. The "right" here isn't just to add emphasis; it also makes the expression sound more polite, as it highlights the speaker's eagerness to accommodate the other person.

私はここで、何とかして次の2つの場面をカバーするフレーズを考案しようとしました。出入り口を通り抜けるときなどに人に先に進んでよいと許可を与える場合と、人に食べ物などを取ってよいと許可を与える場合です。**Go right ahead.** と **Please go ahead.** で迷ったのですが、それは後者だと2語の表現に単に **please** を足して3語にすることになり、それでは本書の3語フレーズの方針に反するように思えるからです。結局、**Go right ahead.** が正解だと判断しました。この **right** は単に強調のためだけのものでなく、表現により丁寧な響きを添えます。相手に便宜を図りたいという話し手の気持ちを強調するからです。

「万歳！」

138

"I [We/You/He/She/They] **did it!**"

「やったー！」

文で説明してみよう！

Although **"Banzai!"** literally translates to "10,000 years of life," it's often used as a cheer or battle cry.

「万歳！」は直訳すると「1万年の人生」だが、たいてい応援や戦いの掛け声として使われる。

3 語フレーズを会話で使おう！

Noah jumped up on his desk, screaming, **"I did it!"** when he was told he was elected student government president.

ノアは、生徒会長に選ばれたことを知らされると、机の上に飛び乗って「万歳！」と叫びました。

Andrew's Point

Without a deep dive into Japanese culture, it would be difficult to explain in three words how a cry of triumph is related to 10,000 years. "We did it!" lacks depth but it does a satisfactory job of conveying enthusiasm in a number of situations, including sports events and meeting sales quotas. One other thing the English does not do is explain the word's relation to miniature potted trees. Yes, many people confuse both the spelling and the pronunciation of "banzai" and "bonsai." I wonder what people will say when I cry out, "Miniature potted trees!" the next time my soccer team wins a match.

日本文化を深く掘り下げない限り、1万年の歴史とつながる勝利の雄叫びを3語で説明するのは難しいでしょう。**We did it!**には深みがありませんが、スポーツ大会や営業ノルマの達成など、数々の場面での熱狂を伝える役割は十分果たします。一つ、この英語が果たせていない役割があります。この言葉と小型の鉢植えの関係を説明することです。そう、多くの人が「バンザイ」と「盆栽」のつづりと発音の両方を混同しているのです。今度、私のサッカーチームが試合に勝ったとき、私が**Miniature potted trees!**と叫んだら、みんな何と言うでしょうか。

「もったいない」

139

"What a waste!"

「何という無駄なのか！」

 文で説明してみよう！

"Mottainai." is a concept rooted in Buddhist doctrine that conveys a sense of sadness or shame when an item that still has potential use goes to waste.

「もったいない」とは、仏教の教義に根ざした概念で、まだ使えるものが無駄になることの悲しさや後ろめたさを表している。

 3語フレーズを会話で使おう！

"What a waste!" I exclaimed as my baby slapped her food onto the floor.

「もったいない！」と私は叫びました。自分の赤ん坊が食べ物を床にたたきつけたからです。

Andrew's Point

The most natural way to express a sense of shame in English when something goes to waste is to say, "What a waste!" There is, however, no functional equivalent of the "Mottainai Obake" that lends me a helping, ghostly hand to stop my kids from wasting water or leaving extra food on their plates. The Japanese term "mottainai," while not yet globally understood, has appeared outside of Japan in various contexts. Kenyan environmentalist and Nobel Prize winner Wangari Maathai introduced the word as a slogan for environmental protection when addressing the U.N. She said that it encompasses the four Rs of reduce, reuse, recycle, and repair. She also had it written on a t-shirt.

何かが無駄になってしまったときに、その後ろめたさを英語で表現する最も自然な方法は、**What a waste!** と言うことです。しかし、「もったいないお化け」に相当するものは英語にはありません。このお化けは、子供たちが水を無駄にしたり、皿に食べ物を残したりしないように、幽霊のように手を貸してくれるのです。日本語の「もったいない」という言葉は、まだ全世界で理解されているわけではありませんが、日本以外の国でもさまざまな文脈で取り上げられてきました。ケニアの環境保護活動家でノーベル賞受賞者のワンガリ・マータイさんは、国連でこの言葉を環境保護のスローガンとして紹介しました。彼女いわく、この言葉は4つの**R**、つまり **reduce**（削減）、**reuse**（再使用）、**recycle**（リサイクル）、**repair**（修理）を包含しているとのことです。彼女はTシャツにもこの言葉をプリントしていました。

索引